A BISCUIT FOR YOUR SHOE:
A Memoir of County Line, a Texas Freedom Colony

by
BEATRICE UPSHAW

Introduction and Photos by
Richard Orton

Texas Folklore Society Extra Book Number 28

University of North Texas Press

Denton, Texas

10 9 8 7 6 5 4 3 2 1

Permissions:
University of North Texas Press
1155 Union Circle #311336
Denton, TX 76203-5017

The paper used in this book meets the minimum requirements of the American
National Standard for Permanence of Paper for Printed Library Materials,
z39.48.1984. Binding materials have been chosen for durability.

Library of Congress Cataloging-in-Publication Data

Names: Upshaw, Beatrice, 1958- author. | Orton, Richard S., 1946- writer of
    introduction, photographer (expression)
Title: A biscuit for your shoe : a memoir of County Line, a Texas freedom
    colony / by Beatrice Upshaw ; introduction and photos by Richard Orton.
Other titles: Texas Folklore Society extra book ; no. 28.
Description: Denton, Texas : University of North Texas Press, [2020] |
    Series: Texas Folklore Society extra book ; number 28 | Includes index.
    | Summary: "Book is a memoir of growing up in the East Texas freedom
    colony, County Line. There is an introduction and foreword that offer
    context, and photographs"-- Provided by publisher.
Identifiers: LCCN 2020034080 | ISBN 9781574418125 (cloth) | ISBN
    9781574418217 (ebook)
Subjects: LCSH: Upshaw, Beatrice, 1958- | Upshaw family. | Community
    life--Texas--County Line (Nacogdoches County) | African
    Americans--Colonization--Texas--County Line (Nacogdoches County) |
    Freedmen--Colonization--Texas--County Line (Nacogdoches County) | County
    Line (Nacogdoches County, Tex.)--Biography. | County Line (Nacogdoches
    County, Tex.)--Social life and customs--20th century. | LCGFT:
    Autobiographies.
Classification: LCC F394.C8125 U67 2020 | DDC 976.4/182063--dc23
LC record available at https://lccn.loc.gov/2020034080

A Biscuit for Your Shoe: A Memoir of County Line, a Texas Freedom Colony
is Texas Folklore Society Extra Book Number 28

The electronic edition of this book was made possible by the support
of the Vick Family Foundation.

CONTENTS

FOREWORD

Frances B. Vick

The publication of this Number Twenty-Eight: Texas Folklore Society Extra Book is the first publication out of our new home at Tarleton State University. The Society is ensconced in our new quarters and delighted to be here. We are extremely grateful to finally have arrived and look forward to this new partnership for the Texas Folklore Society. The joining of these two institutions— Tarleton State University and the Texas Folklore Society—will be an opportunity for both organizations to preserve Texas Folklore, history and culture.

We will also have access to the Dora Lee Langdon Cultural & Educational Center in Granbury, Texas, part of a full city block. A bit of history to acquaint you with the site we are anxious for you to visit:

> The Dora Lee Langdon Cultural & Educational Center is to extend the reach of Tarleton State University in cooperation with the City of Granbury by developing and maintaining relationships with a broader constituency, to enhance the public image of the University and City through quality cultural programs and to encourage life-long learning through community education opportunities.

With this move, the Texas Folklore Society joyfully becomes part of the communities of Tarleton State University, the Langdon

Center, the City of Granbury, Hood County and not far from the city of Fort Worth.

In trading the majestic pines of my East Texas roots for the wide-open vistas of Central Texas, the Texas Folklore Society has an opportunity to recalibrate our mission and renew our vision to build an intentional highway to the future through the study of and appreciation for Texas Folklore.

Our co-founder, John A. Lomax, spent his first year off the farm in college in Granbury. Our patron saint, J. Frank Dobie, the first Secretary/Editor of the Texas Folklore Society, was the one who put the first Mexican woman in a place of honor when he named Jovita Gonzalez, one of my heroines, President of the Texas Folklore Society in 1930–31 and again 1931–32. I feel pretty certain that he would not be too upset or surprised that the Texas Folklore Society has seen fit to name a first female Secretary/Editor with this move to Tarleton State University. I will repeat here what I wrote to you Paisanos upon receiving the news of the vote that elected me:

> Dear Paisanos,
>
> I am overwhelmed and humbled by the honor bestowed on me by the TFS Board and by your vote agreeing with their choice. I will endeavor to not fail you in this position until a permanent replacement can be found.
>
> I have been amazed at the incredible work done by this board and the past board presidents: Elaine Davenport, Past President; Sarana Savage, Immediate Past President; Lori Najar, President; Kay Arnold, Vice President; Patrick Vick, Treasurer; Board Members: Rollo K. Newsom, Acayla Haile, Phyllis Bridges; Carol Hanson, Chuck Smith, Scott Bumgardner, Jim Bridges, Lorraine Mason, Mary Harris and Blaine Williams.

Thank all of you Paisanos for trusting me. I promise to do my best to not let you down.

In your service
Frances Brannen Vick
Secretary/Editor
Texas Folklore Society

As I write this, we are in the middle of a world-wide pandemic caused by coronavirus. More than ever, even as the coronavirus pandemic continues to infect our world, we can look to our past to see how our ancestors overcame trials such as these. Global diseases and Great Recessions are accounted for in the annals of history and folklore. Working together we can and will get through these trying times to put our lives back together and keep the Texas Folklore Society not only relevant, but vibrant, healthy and growing.

In your service

Frances Brannen Vick

John and Lucy
UPSHAW
Family Tree

b. = born, d. = died, s: = spouse, p: = partner

John Upshaw   Lucy _____
b. 1825 TN   b. 1827 GA

1. ALEXANDER UPSHAW
    b. 1850 MS

2. AUGUSTUS "GUSS" UPSHAW
    b. 12 Mar 1851 TX
    d. 23 Dec 1914 TX
    s: Elmyra "Ella" Mathis/Matthews
        b. 08 May 1867 TX
        d. 08 Feb 1946 TX
    Child(ren): Wilton Upshaw
                b. 16 Nov 1884 TX
                d. 28 Feb 1961 CA
                s: Ida Simmons
                Child(ren): Carrie Upshaw
                            b. 1903 TX

    ❖ ANNA BELLE UPSHAW
        b. 29 Jan 1886 TX
        d. 15 May 1969 TX
        s: J. S. Starks

    ❖ HADIE UPSHAW
        b. 09 Oct 1887 TX
        d. 21 Sept 1972 TX
        p: Lola Upshaw
        Child(ren): Willie D. "Bo" Upshaw   b. 26 Sept 1930 TX/
                                                       20 Jul 1997 TX

                    Thelma B. Upshaw   b. 1938 TX
                    Erlene Upshaw   b. Unknown TX
                    Joyce Faye Upshaw   b. 19 Jan 1946 TX/
                                                       20 Sept 2019 TX

                    Evia Lois Upshaw   b. Unknown TX
                    Aline Upshaw   b. Unknown TX

    ❖ CLARENCE UPSHAW
        b. 1889 TX
        d. Unknown

❖ D. C. UPSHAW
  b. 09 Oct 1890 TX
  d. 29 Dec 1968 CA
  s: Alice Richard
  Child(ren): Bertha Upshaw   b. 1917 TX

❖ WALTER EDDIE UPSHAW
  b. 02 Jul 1892 TX
  d. 19 Apr 1987 CA
  s: Minnie Ola "Mineola" Connor
  Child(ren): Quilla Upshaw   b. Unknown
                         d. 1993

❖ LOUISIANA A. UPSHAW
  b. 23 Nov 1893 TX
  d. 05 Mar 1976 TX
  s: Elson Ross
  Child(ren): Leon Ross   b. 1912 TX
             Claudie Mae Ross b. 1924 TX
             Ruth Hazel Ross b. 1927 TX
             Cleveland Ross b. 1928 TX
             Mamie Ross b. 1929 TX
             Harrell Lamar Ross b. 1932 TX
             Dorothy Ross b. 1935 TX
             Ruby Nell Ross b. 1938 TX

❖ JEFFIE UPSHAW
  b. 22 Nov 1895 TX
  d. 14 Feb 2003 TX
  s: B. B. Ross
  Child(ren): Esau Hennon Ross b. 1922 TX
             Gladys M. Ross b. 1933 TX

❖ LUTHER UPSHAW
  b. 19 Mar 1896 TX
  d. 28 Dec 1986 CA
  s. Elelia Smith
  Child(ren): Audie Lee Upshaw b. 1923 TX
             Littleton Upshaw b. 1925 TX
             Lee Vernon "Giddy" Upshaw b. 1927 TX

❖ NEAL "N. E." UPSHAW
   b. 24 Apr 1899 TX
   d. 02 May 1997 TX
   s: Velma Brown
   Child(ren): Mirtle L. Upshaw   b. 1925 TX
               Colester Upshaw   b. 1927 TX
               Flora Dean Upshaw   b. 1928 TX
               Leonard Upshaw   b. 1929 TX
               Ruby Upshaw   b. 1931 TX
               Marion Nell Upshaw   b. 1933 TX
               Dolvin Alonzo Upshaw   b. 1935 TX
               Doil Upshaw   b. 1935 TX
               Luther Ravory Upshaw   b. 1938 TX
               Travis Upshaw   b. 1940 TX
               Anita Louise Upshaw   b. 1942 TX
               Eisenhower Upshaw   b. 1945 TX
               Ella Fay Upshaw   b. 1946 TX
               Fredrick Mccurdy Upshaw   b. 1948 TX

❖ LAURA J. UPSHAW
   b. 1900 TX
   d. Unknown

❖ RACHEL UPSHAW
   b. 04 May 1902 TX
   d. 18 Jul 1927 TX

❖ CLAUDE UPSHAW
   b. 17 Nov 1904 TX
   d. 06 Jul 1975 TX
   s: Idell _____
   s: Carrie Esco
   Child(ren): Claude Upshaw Jr.   b. 1925 TX
                                            d. 1984 KY
               Roy "R. C." Upshaw   b. 1928 TX

❖ FLOYD UPSHAW
   b. 27 Apr 1905 TX
   d. 31 Aug 1986 TX
   s: Bea _____
   s: Odessa Waters

❖ ROOSEVELT UPSHAW
   b.   13 Apr 1906 TX
   d.   06 Apr 1963 CA
   s: Alameda _____

❖ BAKER UPSHAW
   b.   1908 TX
   d.   Unknown

❖ EDWARD MONEL UPSHAW
   b.   01 May 1909 TX
   d.   15 Jul 2002 TX
   s: Leota Ruelene Freeman

Child(ren):	
Eddie James Skinner	b. 18 Mar 1935 TX
	d. 28 Aug 2004 TX
Demorris Evalene Upshaw	b. 22 Nov 1936 TX
Ruth Hazel Skinner	b. 19 May 1938 TX
Claude Ivy "Bubba" Upshaw	b. 12 Jun 1940 TX
Maye Florence Upshaw	b. 22 Apr 1942 TX
	d. 22 Jan 2017 TX
Eugene "Gene" Upshaw	b. 25 Nov 1943 TX
Faye Eddie Upshaw	b. 12 Oct 1945 TX
Marceline "Byrd" Upshaw	b. 30 Apr 1947 TX
Alfred Clark "Tenchie" Upshaw	b. 19 Apr 1951 TX
	d. 24 Mar 2006 CA
Alvin Langston "Pete" Upshaw	b. 26 Feb 1953 TX
Marilyn Ruelene "Sister Girl" Upshaw	b. 17 Aug 1955 TX
Beatrice Ann "Slang" Upshaw	b. 17 May 1958 TX
Gus Edward Upshaw	b. 20 Dec 1959 TX

❖ ODELL UPSHAW
   b.   18 Feb 1914 TX
   d.   15 Jun 1987 CA

3. FELIX UPSHAW
   b. 1856 TX
   d. Unknown
   s: Bettie Bailey
   Child(ren): James "Lil Jim" Upshaw   b. 1877 TX
        d. 1948 TX

   Tennessee Upshaw   b. 1880 TX
        d. 09 Nov 1958 TX

   s: Mary Anderson
   Child(ren): Addie Upshaw   b. 1887 TX
        Mattie Upshaw   b. 1890 TX
        John Upshaw   b. 14 Feb 1892 TX
        d. 26 Aug 1969 TX

        Ida Rine Upshaw   b. 05 Jul 1895
        d. 21 Apr 1949 TX

        Earnest Upshaw   b. 1898 TX
        d. 10 Apr 1974 CA

        Dorsey Upshaw   b. 20 Feb 1900
        d. 01 May 1960 TX

        Earl "Ural" Upshaw   b. 06 Apr 1903 TX
        d. 13 Jan 1976 TX

        Pearlina "Pearl" Upshaw   b. 07 Mar 1906 TX
        d. 26 Sept 1972 TX

4. JAMES "BIG JIM" UPSHAW
   b. 03 Apr 1858 TX
   d. 24 Apr 1932 TX
   p: Martha Whitaker
   Child(ren): Clinton "Clint" Upshaw   b. 01 Mar 1882 TX
        d. 29 May 1956 TX

   s: Laura Tinsley
   Child(ren): Zuella Upshaw   b. 09 Nov 1884 TX
        d. 06 Mar 1976 TX

        Eugene Leonard Upshaw   b. 31 Oct 1886 TX
        d. 24 May 1968 NY

        John Gillis Upshaw   b. 12 Aug 1888 TX
        d. 04 May 1968 CA

        Luvenia Upshaw   b. 10 Sept 1890 TX
        d. 05 Sept 1980 TX

5. DOC UPSHAW
   b. 1860 TX
   d. Unknown

INTRODUCTION

A long time ago, or so it seems, I went to County Line for the first time and met the Upshaw family. County Line, also known as the Upshaw Community, is in northwest Nacogdoches County in Deep East Texas. That was 1988. I was looking for a photo project to do in East Texas while visiting my parents in Nacogdoches.

A family friend, Professor F. E. "Ab" Abernethy, told me about African American land-owner communities dating from the Emancipation. I was beyond surprised when Ab told me that such communities existed . . . places established by emancipated African Americans on land they owned! My Texas and American history schooling didn't tell that story when I was growing up.

Ab introduced me to Marion Upshaw, born and raised in County Line. Marion taught school in Nacogdoches for many years and was an administrator in the Nacogdoches Independent School District when we met.

As Thad Sitton wrote in the Foreword to my book, *The Upshaws of County Line: An American Family:*

> Freedmen's settlements like County Line were independent communities of African American landowners and land squatters that formed in the eastern half of Texas during the years after Emancipation in 1865. Similar places took root in other former slave states. These "freedom colonies," as black people sometimes called them, were anomalies in a post-war South where whites quickly resumed social, economic, and political control, and the agricultural system of sharecropping came to dominate.
>
> Freedmen's strong desires for land, autonomy, and isolation from whites motivated formation of these independent black communities. After the 1865 rumor that the federal government soon would provide all ex-slaves with "forty acres and a mule" proved false, most freed persons remained in the countryside and took employments with white

landowners as day laborers, sharecroppers, or share tenants. Another large group of ex-slaves moved to segregated quarters adjacent to white towns. But a minority of former bondsmen set out to get their forty acres and a mule quite on their own, and a good many of them succeeded.

It was lonely out there in the white countryside, so a lot of these people formed dispersed farming communities— "settlements," Southerners often called them, whether blacks or whites resided there—places un-platted and unincorporated, individually unified only by church and school and residents' belief that a community existed.

My curiosity took me to County Line, at Marion's invitation, the day after Thanksgiving in 1988.

There I met his uncle and aunt, Edward Monel and Leota Ruelene Freeman Upshaw, otherwise known as "Butch" and "Oti," and they agreed to let me to come to their home, make photographs anywhere I wanted in the community, and learn about the history of County Line. I will never understand why they agreed to this so readily, but their decision changed my life fundamentally.

Beatrice Upshaw is the twelfth of the thirteen children raised by Monel and Leota. In the early '90s she gave me a manuscript of her personal memoir about growing up in County Line that she called "A Biscuit for Your Shoe." Like other experiences I'd had in County Line, reading "Biscuit" connected me to experiences outside my own, and yet oddly familiar.

For example, here is how her story about her Uncle Claude's store in County Line begins:

> The general store was by far the most popular hang-out in our small, close-knit rural community. Well, really it was the only hang-out unless you counted the church that was situated just across the road.

It seemed sacrilegious to think of County Line Missionary Baptist Church as a hangout, so we never considered our church in that light. It probably would have been all right for the Southern Baptists, but the Missionary Baptists hold themselves to less lenient standards.

It was not to the church that we turned for basic entertainment. Rather, the store was *the* place to be on Saturday. Community residents hung out at the store morning, noon and night. My paternal uncle, Claude Upshaw, owned and operated the general store. He had an ancient black and white RCA television, surely the prototype, and an even older brown, plastic tabletop Philco radio. That's it. There was no jukebox, no pool table, no dance floor, no record player. Likewise, there were no magazines, newspapers, or comic books. There was nothing to draw people to the store except amiable fellowship and innocuous amusement. The eclectic selection of stocked groceries and dry goods was an added bonus, an excuse to go to the store even if there was no real need.

And in another story, she recounts her early memories of the "All Night Singing":

The days passed swiftly from the time school dismissed in May until the first big event of the summer. The All-Night Singing was held on the second Saturday night in July. It is an annual event, which for school-aged children signals the mid-point of summer vacation.

For the occasion, neighbors and local church members were invited to spend the evening with our church family, singing and praising the Lord. Sometimes the singing went on until well after midnight, thus the title of the event. This was a time of great excitement for us kids. There was not a lot else to do and we could only spend so much time hanging out at the store. Going to church was a great social occasion.

Places with origins similar to County Line still exist all over East Texas and the rest of the South. Not all emancipated African Americans became sharecroppers and domestics. Some of them started their own communities separate from whites, and many of them were out in the countryside where they had more autonomy.

As a result, daily life in places we now call "Freedom Colonies" was often somewhat free of the white judgement and approval (and of the possible consequences) in Jim Crow America. The community provided for all its basic needs by farming and by fishing in the Angelina River in the beginning.

And they had to clear the land, a wilderness just east of the river. I can't imagine doing that myself, but I have no trouble understanding the motivation behind it. They went from slavery to landowner in a few years. Land ownership was the certificate of real freedom for a freedman.

Freedom Colonies generally had a church at the center of their community. The County Line Baptist Church came into being in 1896. In the 1996 Celebrating One Hundred Years church event program (and in her book as well) Beatrice Upshaw wrote:

> County Line Baptist Church was established in the 1890s. It began as a modest frame structure. It was located just above the bend in the road on the north side of Aunt LA's home. Rumor had it that the original burned to the ground when a visiting neighbor started a big fire in the wood heater. The fire became much bigger than he ever intended.
>
> Anyway, after this building burned, a new church was constructed about a hundred yards away. It was on the same road but closer to the middle of the community, just across

from Uncle Claude's store. It, too, was a modest frame building, considerably less modest than the original one.

Before 1896, the Upshaws attended the Stonewall Baptist Church,
just west of Douglass on Hwy. 21. The Stonewall Cemetery, well
behind that church and off the highway, is still the County Line
cemetery where the original settlers are buried along with their
descendants.

Grave of Guss and Ella Upshaw in Stonewall Cemetery

County Line had its own school by the early 1900s. During the first decade of the 20th century the school employed E. J. Campbell and his wife, Mary, to teach their children. Raised in County Line by his aunt, Ella Mathis Upshaw, Campbell later became a prominent citizen of Nacogdoches, where he was appointed principal of the Nacogdoches Colored School in 1910.

These two institutions, the church and the school, formed the cultural center of the community. Spirituality and education were fundamental to survival and freedom in Post-Emancipation times. In communities like County Line the founders had the agency to establish and maintain these institutions.

The Upshaw brothers, Guss, Felix and Jim, with their families, founded County Line in the 1870s, most likely as squatters in the beginning, but by the turn of the century the Upshaws held title to around 600 acres in northwest Nacogdoches County a few miles from the town of Douglass.

Guss, Felix, and Jim were born as slaves and emancipated as children, and they had important skills along with a level of motivation that, with endless hard work, enabled them to be successful in establishing and maintaining a new community.

The only Upshaws in Nacogdoches County in the 1870 census lived in Douglass. John Upshaw, 45 and born in Tennessee, and Lucy, 43 and born in Georgia, had five children in their household: Alexander, 19 and born in Mississippi, Guss, 19, Felix, 14, James, 12, and Doc, 10 . . . all born in Texas.

In 1875, John Upshaw borrowed $75 in gold from L. C. Whitaker for the purpose of growing his own crop of cotton and corn on Whitaker's land. This loan was recorded at the Nacogdoches County Court House. As collateral John offered "one brown mare mule, one Sorrel mare, one wagon and my crop of corn and cotton that I may raise and cultivate for the present year 1875 upon L. C. Whitaker's farm in Nacogdoches County."

In 1876, Guss, then in his mid-20s, bought an 80-acre tract of land three miles west of Douglass that he sold several years later. It's not clear when the three Upshaw brothers settled in what came to be known as County Line. This likely occurred in the late 1870s or early 1880s. The first deeds recorded for their land were in 1887 (Felix), 1889 (James), and 1890 (Guss). Members of the Upshaw family continued to purchase land in the area, incurring debt which they paid on schedule. In 1906, the three brothers all sold timber leases for their land.

Leonard Upshaw, a grandson of Guss and Ella, describes Guss as follows:

> Farming, fishing, basket weaving, logging wagon repair, blacksmithing, and animal raising were most of his hobbies and occupations. He had a fish trap on the Angelina and sold fish by the wagon loads in neighboring communities.

According to family lore, Guss could weave a basket that would hold water. Felix spent his time farming. Jim, the youngest of the brothers, built a mill that ground corn, ginned cotton, and milled timber. He and his wife, Laura, gave the Upshaw Common School District #62 two acres of land in 1915, and in 1920, they gave County Line Missionary Baptist Church the land on which the church now stands. According to Jeffrey Roth and J. B. Watson:

> In 1915 [Upshaw] needed a new school and the people of County Line resurveyed the boundaries of taxable properties within Upshaw Common School District number 62. They then petitioned the Nacogdoches County Commissioners Court for the right to tax their own property within the survey boundary to issue county bonds to buy property, build and equip a school.

The citizens of County Line, an unincorporated community in the East Texas wilderness . . . when left to their own devices to educate their children, asked for permission to tax *themselves* to make a good school in their community!

This bit of history helps clarify the significance of freedom colonies in the context of the time. In varying degrees, many of them had the agency to control their lives for the most part. They were landowners. Their school and church melded together children, parents, teachers, and the community at large. When it came, desegregation was, ironically, a mixed blessing. In County Line the school was part of the community in the most direct and intimate sense. It was the neighborhood school, and there was only one neighborhood in County Line.

Desegregation brought an end to their neighborhood school. When County Line children went to Cushing and Nacogdoches for school, their parents no longer had any connection with their school or teachers. Almost all of their children's teachers were now white . . . and no real connection existed between the community and the school.

Other communities had their own connection issues after desegregation. The Dixie Community in Jasper County lost their school when desegregation occurred, but they got it back many years later when the property was put on sale. Fred McCray states:

> Our family sits down and we talk a lot and we share some visions, and one of those visions was that if the property that used to house our elementary school . . . if that property ever became available we would do what we could to get that property back into our community. . . . It went on the market in 2014 and we put our vision into action to get it back into the community. We succeeded, realizing we could really do something to advance our youth and to also do some things

to preserve the history of our community. That's how we got started on the project. We decided that once we actually acquired the facility we would do whatever we could to bring families together.

Fred McCray was born and raised in the Dixie Community, Jasper County, a couple of hours south and east of County Line. His family and several others bought their old school building and property from segregation days and converted the buildings into event and meeting centers focused on re-establishing a sense of community in the Dixie Community. They named it the Connection Center.

The Connection Center is a hub for the Dixie Community. It is re-connecting what had become a slightly disconnected community, doing it by producing various events and programs and by making the facility available for others to use in the surrounding area. It is the product of a concerted effort from a large core of older members of the community to re-claim their heritage and make a place to remember and preserve that heritage.

Regarding the community, Bobby Joe Hadnot writes:

> My granddad, Albert McCray, was the oldest of four children raised without a father, and they lived on white folks' land and he was very respected by people that knew him because of his work ethic and his ability to be creative. I call him a chemist because he could make syrup, he could take stuff from the farm and make other things out of it, and he didn't only do it for himself, but he helped other people in the community.... Today, I butcher hogs. I'm doing it now because I want to pass it on. Growing up and observing how he did it . . . its so amazing to me."

Bobby Joe Hadnot was instrumental in acquiring the old school and property, the Connection Center.

Fred McCray's ongoing commitment to the community and the Connection Center no doubt comes from feelings such as these. He states:

> I just feel so strongly about the community that I was raised in. I know I heard when I was growing . . . and it's not an abstraction . . . "It takes a village." When I was growing up in this particular community it really was a village. We could depend on any other family in the community if we needed any kind of assistance. And they felt the same way about our family.
>
> I'll tell you what I feel happened in our family. We were taught to respect ourselves, and if you respected yourself other people were likely to respect you. That was one of our foundational learning experiences . . . always respect yourself and treat people the way you would like to be treated.

Many surviving freedom colonies no longer have the resources or energy required to create and sustain such an effort. Some do. And they all face the same questions: What must we do to keep our history alive? What will happen when the last generation to be born and raised in our community is gone? How will we keep our land?

A Biscuit for Your Shoe promotes the first objective, telling about the generation emerging in the Forties, Fifties and beyond. By recounting numerous experiences growing up in County Line as a child, Beatrice Upshaw not only conveys a strong sense of place, but tells us a lot about her community as intimately connected families growing out of unique origins.

The community of Shankleville in Newton County began looking for answers several decades ago. In 1988, descendants of the founders of the freedom colony of Shankleville founded the

Shankleville Historical Society . . . and this is the Shankleville creation story:

> Shankleville is named for Jim and Winnie Shankle, known
> as the first blacks in Newton County, Texas to buy land and
> become local leaders after gaining freedom by emancipation.
> Both were born in slavery: Jim in 1811, Winnie in 1814. After
> Winnie and her three children were sold to a Texan, Jim ran
> away from his Mississippi owner. He traveled by night, for-
> aged for food, swam streams (including the Mississippi River),
> walking out of sight the 400 miles to East Texas. At dusk one
> day he found Winnie beside her master's spring. After slip-
> ping out food for several days, Winnie told her master, who
> arranged to buy Jim. The couple worked side by side, bringing
> up Winnie's children and six of their own. . . . In 1867, they
> began buying land, and with their associate, Steve McBride,
> eventually owned over 4,000 acres.

Today, descendants of Jim and Winnie Shankle concern themselves with keeping their land and maintaining their heritage,
concerns common to black communities throughout East Texas.

The Shankleville Historical Society raises money for scholar-
ships and sponsors reunions and workshops. They are well into
the restoration of an old homestead with outbuildings. They have
done archeology work near the spring mentioned in their creation
story. And there is the Purple Hull Pea Festival held annually in
June to celebrate all things purple hull pea! And from the Purple
Hull Pea Festival emerged an annual symposium on Freedom
Colonies, now in partnership with Prairie View A&M University,
an historical Black university.

The preservation of community and heritage can take various forms. Beatrice Upshaw lives in County Line along with several siblings and cousins. Her daughter and son-in-law live there,

too. One of her cousins built a house in County Line several years ago, and more recently bought and converted an old vacant property a few miles away in Douglass into a combination barbecue restaurant, small grocery, deli, and chocolatery (with Beatrice as chocolatier).

Uncle Doug's emerged from several years of planning initiated and funded by the above-mentioned cousin (descended, as is Beatrice, from Guss and Ella Upshaw) and with input from members of the extended Upshaw family. The creation of Uncle Doug's was and is a family operation honoring a common heritage . . . a heritage testifying to the will and determination of the founders who shaped their portion of the Angelina River Bottom wilderness into a community of their own almost 140 years ago. Could this type of enterprise—Uncle Doug's—be a way for descendants of the community to keep it alive, even though Uncle Doug's is six or seven miles from the community itself?

In its own way Uncle Doug's is cousin to the Connection Center and the Shankleville Historical Society. Each is the result of human resilience and the will to succeed at any cost . . . refusal to be defeated by prejudice.

The Texas Freedom Colony Project, founded by Dr. Andrea Roberts, Asst. Professor of Landscape Architecture and Urban Planning at Texas A&M, aims to create a database of Freedom Colonies throughout Texas. This database would make concrete the existence of places, some now gone, that never had any "legal" existence since they were unincorporated. Such a database would serve as basis for further research about these real "places" that have been largely unacknowledged in our history books. Dr. Roberts' work encompasses six general areas relevant to today's freedom colonies: 1) Land Loss & Dispossession, 2) Environmental Justice, 3) Historic Preservation, 4) Intrusive Infrastructure Projects, 5) Gentrification, and 6) Sustainable Development.

In our supposed admiration of entrepreneurs, self-starters, and the up-from-the-bootstraps culture we think we live in, we have managed to ignore the success of these cultural underdogs— emancipated African Americans and their descendants in today's world.

Beatrice writes, "The fact that our ancestors were able to establish and build a church fresh out of slavery and that we are able to maintain and improve it is a tribute to them, not to us. We are what we are because of what they were made of." Her daughter, Elia Upshaw Ali, states:

> County Line is not a utopian place where all the little Negroes came together and built this community. That's not it. It was a struggle the whole time living there in coming to terms with who I was as a person. It's a beautiful place, it's a lovely place, but it is a place of struggle. Why would anyone want to live there? [The founders] carved this place, this culture, this history out of something that no one else really saw. We made it our own. The people before me made it their own.

Many (most?) of the people working to sustain their community's heritage no longer live in the community. Some of them grew up elsewhere and spent quality time there when they came back to visit, often in the summer. Some of them have moved back or made homes there. What would motivate people to come back and live in places long past their former vitality? What is the nature of the attraction?

I imagine that the people who come back to stay or to visit do so because of good memories . . . because they feel safe there . . . because they are among "their own." And perhaps they all remember, in their own way, the "old people" that Beatrice tells us about . . . and have their own stories to tell.

In *A Biscuit for Your Shoe* Beatrice Upshaw shares her experiences growing up in a self-contained community of extended family beginning in the 1960s, a community established by emancipated slaves in the 1870s and 1880s. Her stories manage to be individual and universal at the same time, sharing close relationships with aunts, uncles, siblings, and parents; the hijinks of children and their ability to create their own amusements and toys; and always told with a sense of humor. Our common humanity is always present in her remembrances.

Richard Orton
Nacogdoches, Texas
January 7, 2020

Richard Orton, visiting with Dolvin Upshaw

CHAPTER 1: RURAL EAST TEXAS

Dinner on the Grounds, County Line Baptist Church

Growing up in rural deep East Texas certainly made for an interesting rearing, though for many years this fact went unrecognized and unappreciated, and I now realize just how good we had it. There are few places today where children can roam freely without so much as a passing thought to what evils could befall them.

There were no evils then, not in our corner of the universe. We were shrouded in ignorant bliss concerning what went on outside our haven. Far and away from us was the worry of drive-by shootings, drug busts, robberies, and murders. Some of the terminology heard frequently today describing the state of our nation had not even been coined back then. We were innocent, naïve, country folks who largely made up the backbone of the nation—*then*.

The most excitement we country bumpkins experienced outside the community was visiting the annual state fair in Dallas. Each fall during our junior and senior high school years, we loaded onto two giant yellow school buses and made the three-hour journey from County Line to Dallas. The day was filled with fun and adventure, a day we were glad to experience, and just as glad to have end. The city was wonderful . . . for a while.

Many of us visited the city for entire summers, spending the time with relatives who had relocated. Still, we had little concept at the time of our fortune in having been so sheltered by country living. The passage of time and intense exposure to the rest of the world would eventually open our eyes to what has become a different lifestyle.

We were insulated against most of life's horrors. We saw the police or local sheriff rarely. When the "law" came around they were generally in search of new hunting territory. The game they sought was of the edible variety—squirrels, rabbits, deer—not the criminal type. On the rare occasions when they were looking for a criminal, we knew exactly who it was and where to find him.

Compared to today's sophisticated lawbreaker, he was a very small fish indeed.

Illegal drugs and controlled substances were uncommon. It was many years before I knew anyone with an addiction to drugs. It took even longer for me to meet someone who had ever sold them. Even the weed we were familiar with back then was the kind you pulled out of your garden. You burned it in a pile along with other trash, not in a cigarette. The first time we kids saw marijuana was when the school system finally decided to educate us by exposure. It was 1970, and I was twelve years old. Looking at the pictures and small samples of weed left me largely unimpressed. I wasn't using it, I didn't know anyone who was using it, and I had no plans for that to change.

I felt shielded from the dangers of drugs and, to a great extent, alcohol. It just was not an issue in my young life. Of course, there were those who grew up as I did who later experimented with or seriously abused drugs and alcohol. That was bound to happen, but those early years were mostly untainted by such habits.

Our community is a relatively isolated enclave comprising some eight square miles of little-touched woodland. It is situated a mile or so due east of the Angelina River, about twenty miles west of Nacogdoches, Texas. There was only one way into and out of the community. That is unless you wanted to take your chances traversing the river bottom. Several other communities, ranches and farms were nearby, so perhaps secluded is a better word than isolated.

East Texas is rich in natural resources, and timber is king of all. Years ago people there trapped animals for their fur, but that industry has since been played out. In addition to timber, there is oil and natural gas. We were not fortunate enough to have any of either on our property. Every so often oil or gas company surveyors and geologists visited the community. Their purpose was to site likely locations for potential oil exploration.

Community co-founders, Jim and Laura Upshaw (archival)

One time an oil company actually conducted an exploratory drill on our property. First, the geologists determined where the drilling should occur. Then came the surveyors with their plastic ribbons of many colors. They scouted the area for several days,

measuring and calculating, before finally choosing the drilling
site. At their command, big trucks lumbered into the community
hauling their derricks and pumps and other machinery. It took
the crew several days just to get their equipment in place.

One of their first tasks was to dig a giant hole called a "slush
pit." The hole was about thirty feet long by twenty feet wide and
approximately fourteen feet deep. I have no idea what the hole was
for, but after the drillers left, my sister and younger brother and I
spent hours playing in and around it. I know that was not the pit's
purpose.

Heavy rains caused the pit to fill with water. We did not
play near there at such times because of the possibility of getting
snake-bit. Venomous water moccasins are native to the area and
are attracted to the standing water.

After the derrick was set up and operational, there were
weeks and weeks of irritating noise. Boom. Boom. Boom. The dull
thuds of the drilling rig sounded loudly as its bit tore through the
sandy loam, then clay, then rock, tirelessly searching for a sign of
black gold. The noise was horrendous. I was particularly sensitive
to it because I was ill and feverish with bacterial pneumonia when
the drilling started and for the first two weeks of its operation.
That "boom, boom, boom" nearly drove me out of my mind.

My siblings Gus and Marilyn (Sister Girl) visited the site
almost daily. They waited until the crew left for the day before
hiking the hundred yards up the hill. Minutes later they returned
and excitedly updated me on the progress the crew had made.

I was too sick to explore the drilling site until near the end of
the operation. By then the drilling had stopped and almost all of
the equipment had been removed. There was very little to see by
the time I was well enough to see it. The most impressive element
was that big hole in the ground. For several years, until wind and

Gus, circa 1970s

rain erosion filled it in, it was a vivid reminder that something had happened in that spot.

That I was unable to witness the action in vivo was disappointing, but my siblings did a good job of reporting the adventures. Oil exploration was heady stuff, an interesting diversion in our otherwise quiet lives. As long as they were drilling we knew they were still looking, and as long as they were still looking there remained a chance that we could become the Clampetts of East Texas—rich beyond our wildest dreams. I would have made a good Ellie Mae—darkened up a bit.

Sister Girl and I often fantasized about how to spend the vast wealth that would surely be ours once the drillers struck oil. Granny (Mama) would get a new house, one large enough to house her many and varied collections: antiques, children, quilts, more children, linens, and grandchildren. Jed (Butch, our father) would get a new truck, one that could be started with a key rather than a "push start" down the hill.

Unfortunately, the drilling crew found nothing worth sinking a well for. In a way I was glad; the noise from the site was

Marilyn (Sister Girl),
circa 1971

deafening and constant. I was happy when they took down their
equipment and left after finding only minuscule pockets of natural gas. I admit it. Later, I realized how absurd it was to rejoice in
the expedition's failure. I was young at the time and very naïve.

The fantasies faded and reality came roaring back. We were
not going to be rich. We were not going to be the "East Texas
Upshaws" but were destined to remain what we had always been,
the "Upshaws of East Texas." There is, you know, a distinction
between the two.

The business with the oil prospecting was by far the most
interesting and enlightening experience we had involving surveyors. We were always excited when *any* surveyors came around,
whether they were from oil companies or the timber industry.
It was fun watching them set up and operate their equipment.
We never learned what the complicated-looking items did, but
the guys were always tolerant of us. We kept far enough away so
as not to be bothersome but close enough to see everything. It
didn't matter that we knew nothing about what we were watching.
After the first few surveyors came and went we were no longer

awe-struck by them or their equipment. We did not even care what they did. I can admit it now without shame: we wanted what they left behind—tacky plastic ribbons.

The crew tied "guide" ribbons to the limbs of trees to mark various routes through the forest. They used blue or red, and sometimes yellow or orange plastic ribbons. The colorful streamers were about an inch wide and about three feet long. I assume the colors were coded to mean something, but whatever it was it meant nothing to us. We just wanted those ribbons.

We females trekked behind the surveyors, taking a few of the ribbons from carefully selected sites. We did not want the men to lose their way in our woods, so we never took ribbons from two trees in a row.

We actually used those gaudy things to ornament our hair. You can imagine how we looked with our ropy black pigtails tied with three feet of red, yellow, orange, or blue plastic ribbon. Sometimes we used all four hideous colors at the same time. Ugh!

CHAPTER 2: THE HILL

Hills in the area were used for more than amusement. County Line was full of vintage (a much nicer description than *old*) cars and pick-up trucks. Oftentimes, these vehicles were in less than perfect repair. The absolute truth is, they were never in perfect repair and were usually in less than running repair. Some of the cars were even beyond pushing, which is arguably the final stage of life for a car. Some were really pitiful.

My cousin's old '58 Chevy was an excellent example. The car was so rusted out that when it was rainy and the roads were wet and muddy we had to hold your feet up off the floor all the while we were riding. If we did not, our legs and feet would be hopelessly splattered with mud. The floorboard of the car was so eaten with rust that there were holes big enough to put your feet through. If we had a mind to, we could easily look straight down and see the red road underneath. It was eerie to ride in a car with holes in it. I was a little afraid that one day someone would fall through one of the holes and then be run over by the back wheels of the vehicle.

My other fear was that while driving along one evening, my cousin would find that the entire bottom of the car had vanished. There he'd be sitting in the driver's seat driving nothing but a steering wheel with no car attached. I doubt he'd get very far. Eventually, he covered the worn spots in the floor with half-inch plywood. That solved that particular problem. When the car's engine threw a rod a few months afterwards, all its other problems were solved as well. My cousin junked the clunker for scrap metal and bought himself a newer model, fully outfitted with floorboards and everything.

Vehicles were a challenge. Every man in the community was by necessity a shade tree mechanic. When the car or truck would not run, out came the tools. If even the tools could not make it go, out came the boost. I don't mean "boost" as in cables connecting a strong battery to a weak one. I mean "boost" as in a mighty shove down a convenient incline.

There was a small creek just below our house about fifty yards or so down the hill. Getting to the creek required a short walk down a rather steep slope. There was a clear (of weeds and bramble) driveway which ran down the hill. Just before the steep drop-off into the creek, the drive veered to the left. Here the grade began to change, going back uphill again. It was this driveway that we used to push-start vehicles when they refused to crank. We pushed the debilitated and dilapidated cars toward the creek, not into it. The hill was used to help jump-start standard shift vehicles only. This technique did not work with automatic transmissions.

When there was a car or truck that would not start but had potential, its owner marshaled his forces—"all hands on deck" and all that. Generally, it took three adults to push a car or truck. In a pinch it could be done with two adults, or one adult and several children (always plentiful around our place).

Someone usually sat in the driver's seat as the car was being pushed. Sometimes the driver was needed to assist in the initial pushing. With the door open, the would-be driver would help push by leaning heavily against the door frame. Occasionally, the driver was the only one available and would have to push by himself. In this case he had to be fleet of foot indeed in order to jump back into the truck at the proper time. Timing was everything.

As the vehicle traveled down the hill quickly gathering speed, the driver jumped into the truck at the most opportune moment, and put his left foot on the clutch and pressed it quickly to the floor. He then engaged the transmission, switching gears from neutral to first or second, depending on how fast the truck was going. The faster the speed the higher the gear.

The vehicle's speed continued to increase as it moved down the hill. The driver waited until the truck was moving its fastest before trying to start it. First the ignition was turned on, then the clutch was released with a snap. Hopefully, one effort was all it took. If the driver was lucky the engine roared to life on the first try. If not, then the next thing to do was hurriedly ensure that the ignition was indeed turned on. There was nothing more frustrating than to go to such trouble only to have your efforts failed because the switch was not on.

If the first attempt was unsuccessful, the driver still had seventy or eighty yards of driveway left, and so he popped the clutch again and again until the truck started or he ran out of hill. The problem was, every time the clutch was popped the transmission was engaged, thus slowing the truck down. Every time the motor failed to "turn over" and start, precious yards of downhill slope were wasted.

Experienced drivers could determine with the first or second attempt whether the vehicle was likely to start or not. If the driver/ mechanic felt he was unlikely to be successful he wisely rode out the descent and then made the left-turn curve about two-thirds of the way down the hill. This way, he could use the momentum gained during the decline to propel the vehicle onward even after the grade changed from decline to incline.

The driver was then in position to work on his vehicle, making mechanical repairs and adjustments as needed. With help, he could then push the vehicle the fifty or so feet to the crest of the hill and begin again. If the driver was *very* lucky (or mechanically gifted), the truck would start in the traditional manner after being tinkered with.

If the driver found himself at the bottom of the hill with no more room to roll, he had little choice but to either fix the car where it sat, or find a tractor or truck to pull the disabled vehicle back up the incline. Physically pushing a vehicle back up the hill was rarely considered and even more rarely attempted. There was a time or two, though, when this is just what we did with one important modification.

Rather than push the car backwards up the hill, we pushed it around on the left-turn curve and back up the other side instead. It was still uphill-going but the grade was considerably less steep and was easier to navigate. The driveway was substantially longer than the steeper slope, but the extra distance was more than offset by the decreased effort needed to push the car.

Whether the car was pushed or pulled out—depending on how many people were available, how strong they were, and how willing they were to risk their backs—everyone unfortunate enough to be present was pressed into service. Only the very young and the very, very old were exempt from helping to push-start a car when the need arose.

Young children quickly learned not only how to push the car but also how to guide the pushed vehicle down the hill. It was essential that children learned how to pop the clutch most effectively as well. Actually, this was how many of us kids learned to drive. Once the car started we had to continue driving down the incline and back up the other side. It was good practice and a heady rush to zoom down one side of the hill and drift back up the other.

Most of the time the vehicles descended the hill either with a driver actually driving or under the power of other humankind pushing from behind. On one occasion, though, a car actually traveled down the hill of its own volition. Or so it appeared.

Tenchie's 1972 Dodge was his pride and joy. He worked hard for the money to buy the car and, of course, was heart-broken when he left for Vietnam and had to leave it behind. The car should have been the least of his worries. The rest of us were just fine with having the car stay behind, though we were sorry about Tenchie having to go. The Dodge was fast and sporty with nice sleek lines. We loved driving it and did so every chance we got.

One evening I, a veteran driver at thirteen, decided to take the car for a spin. I was a good driver so no one was concerned about my taking the car. The problem was, the car would not start.

I knew better than to try and push the car down the hill by myself. I was not quite strong enough to generate the kind of speed necessary for a push-start. So, after a couple of attempts to crank the car I gave up and got out, disappointed that I would not be driving to the store. After I went back into the house I got busy with other chores and soon forgot all about the car.

Later on that evening, about dusk-dark, Mama, Sister Girl, and I were outside chatting with Aunt Jeffie and her girls. Aunt Jeffie was about to leave, so we were kind of hanging all over the truck delaying her departure. We kids didn't care so much about her leaving but we wanted to visit with our buddies, her grand-daughters, a bit longer.

All of a sudden there was a soft but discernible popping noise. Conversation ceased abruptly as all heads swiveled toward the sound. Dread was almost palpable when a split-second later Tenchie's car began rolling down the hill. My first reaction was, "Oh no!" There were small trees and all kinds of stuff at the bottom of that hill. There was also that steep drop-off into the creek. The car would probably be totaled when it reached the bottom. It certainly would sustain heavy damage.

In a flash of abject stupidity I took off after the car. I don't know what I thought I could do even if I had caught up with it. I guess I envisioned myself a heroine: yanking open the door, jumping in and braking, thus saving the car from crashing into the creek. What would most likely have happened is that I would have gotten tangled up in the door, dragged under the car and killed.

Anyway, none of it happened because I never caught the car. My family stood watching in shock as I ran headlong down the hill. They were so surprised that it was several seconds before anyone even thought to yell at me to stop. Someone, I don't remember who, finally remembered that it was just a car after all and started shouting.

"Stop! Stop, girl!" they yelled.

I, on the other hand, was totally oblivious to the danger I was willing to risk. I could only think about how upset Tenchie would be if he came home and found his car wrecked. I trailed the car for twenty yards or so before I stopped running, acknowledging that there was no way I could catch that car. It was traveling much too fast. I stood watching, cringing inside as I waited for the crashing sound that would signal the end of the Dodge's journey.

Lo and behold! Just as the car reached the edge of the drop-off it stopped, halted by the masses of vines and brush which grew prolifically along the edge of the cliff. The car sat there as if suspended in mid-air. It was eerie the way it just stopped.

Aunt Jeffie later said that she saw something white in the driver's seat—white like a ghost or other specter, that is. I don't much believe in ghosts and haunts. The interior of the car was off-white and it is most likely that's what she saw as the car streaked by. Perhaps the car did start and stop by supernatural forces. I cannot say.

For years, I kept secret the fact that I had even been near the car that day, just hours before the mishap. I never told a soul until now.

Getting the car out proved to be quite a venture, as it was at the very bottom of the hill. There was no possibility of maneuvering it around the curve and back up the low hill on the other side. This car would have to be pulled out, and that is exactly what happened. No, we did not call a tow truck. We were as self-reliant as possible, rarely seeking outside help for problems. Calling a tow truck would have been the last, and I mean *last*, resort.

After securing the car with blocks underneath the front wheels to prevent further movement, Missonnell (a nickname we called our father) hitched a heavy chain to the rear bumper of his half-ton pickup truck. He fastened the other end of the chain to the rear bumper of the Dodge, got under the wheel of his pickup, and began to gun engine. The truck strained and strained but even in its lowest gear, the one most effective for pulling and towing, it could not budge the car. Pete tried dislodging the car by pushing and rocking it but his efforts failed and the truck tires continued to spin, gouging trenches in the soft earth. It was no use. Missonnell's half-ton truck did not have the necessary torque to pull the Dodge up the steep incline.

It happened that our sister Maye and her husband Hadie had been visiting from California during the Christmas season. Maye and Hadie, along with their children, arrived home the day after the Dodge went down the hill. The couple had rented a large cab-over camper for their truck for the journey. The camper added extra weight to their vehicle and turned out to be useful for more than traveling.

The engineering geniuses, my father and brother-in-law, set to work. They hitched the back bumper of Hadie's truck to the front bumper of Butch's truck. Butch's truck's rear bumper was still attached to the Dodge. Heavy chains stretched like umbilical cords between the three vehicles, forming an odd caravan.

Together the two trucks pulled and pulled, strained and groaned. For a while, nothing happened. Then, ever so slowly the Dodge began to disengage from the bramble. I remember thanking God as it inched up the hill that they were able to get it free.

Close inspection revealed no damage to the car. A miracle indeed! Everyone was pleased. I was ecstatic. It might have been my fault after all. Had I gotten out of the car without putting it in gear? I asked myself that question often, but in my heart I believed not. I had lived on that hill all my life; I knew how steep it was. I also knew how important it was to always leave vehicles in the proper gear. It was second nature to gear the transmission and set the parking brake before exiting a car or truck. I believed that I had not left the car in neutral. The popping sound we heard before the car began its descent was most likely the sound of the transmission slipping out of gear.

Leaving the car in first gear obviously was not the wisest course of action; reverse would have been safer, but I was sure I had not left the car in neutral. I had done just as I had intended—to leave the car in what I thought was a safe gear. It apparently slipped out of gear after hours of transmission strain. If it had been in neutral, it would have started rolling as soon as I got out of it.

I consoled myself for months with this reasoning before finally deciding that there are some things we should not try too hard to explain. The more we talk, the more what we say sounds like a lie.

CHAPTER 3: LILBERT

Summers are hot and muggy in East Texas. Temperatures range between 90 and 105 degrees, and humidity is frequently in the range of 70–100%. It can be downright miserable from May until mid-October, but July, August and September are especially uncomfortable. To five foolish young girls out of school for the summer with nothing to do, this heat and humidity simply presented a challenge.

Classes dismissed in mid-May, so we school kids did not have many opportunities to go to Lilbert during summer vacation. And so it was that we—Deborah (Big Sister), Sister Girl, Jeffie Mae, Inez (Chee-Chee), and I—planned to do something exciting that warm July morn. The Fearsome Five decided that we would go to Lilbert for some ice cream, defying the pressing heat and stifling humidity. Uncle Claude had a store and stocked plenty of candy, cookies and soda, but he did not have ice cream.

Lilbert is a small settlement about four miles from our community. The wondrous thing about Lilbert was the two grocery stores, one on either side of the highway. During the school year Mr. Quilla Shears, our bus driver, often stopped at the stores for a few minutes and allowed us to hurry in and buy treats. Everybody got excited when we felt the giant yellow bus slowing to a stop. We rushed in with our nickels and dimes and bought ice cream cones. In those days you could get a very nice sized Borden's ice cream cone for a dime. There were few flavors available: usually only vanilla, chocolate, and strawberry. One or another of the stores carried orange-pineapple, vanilla-chocolate swirl, and perhaps one or two other exotic flavors. The limited variety meant nothing to us. We had never heard of rocky road or jamoca almond fudge ice cream, and frozen yogurt had not been invented yet. We were happy with the choices available.

So, we made up our minds. We were going to Lilbert!

We decided that we would leave home fairly early in the morning to beat the worst of the heat. We chose Aunt Louisiana's (LA's) house as our departure point. We girls met promptly at 9:30 AM. After chatting with our aunt for a few minutes we headed out—Lilbert bound. Aunt LA knew where we were going and did not hesitate to let us know how foolish she thought us. She laughed and wished us luck for our journey.

For the first thirty minutes of our trip we were bursting with energy. We skipped and hopped, played chase and tag, and just had a grand time. We slowed our pace a bit after the first mile and began concentrating on making good time. An hour into the trip and three fourths of the way to our destination we started to fade—quickly. We were young and healthy but were not in particularly good shape, not for long distance hauling, anyway. We had never attempted such a marathon of walking before.

An hour and thirty minutes later we were close enough to Lilbert to have renewed faith that we would indeed make it. We were so confident that we began to play again.

When we got to the graveled road which constituted the final quarter mile of the trip we devised strategies to add more excitement to our journey. Just for fun we idiots lay crosswise in the road with our arms stretched above our heads and tried rolling down the hill. The incline was so slight that it was virtually impossible to roll unless someone helped, so we took turns pushing each other. This would have been pure lunacy anywhere but East Texas. In our neighborhood we could hear traffic coming from miles away. There was very little danger of us getting run over by a car or anything else such as a tractor. There would have been no excuse for getting run over by a tractor as slowly as they traveled.

Suddenly, there was the sound of an approaching vehicle. We got up, those of us being rolled, and began to move toward the edge of the road. We were not in a hurry but there was no sense tempting fate. We walked on slowly, keeping well out of the way of the coming traffic. The urge to play had completely left us by now. We were content to simply put one foot in front of the other and plod along. We still had a lot of walking left.

"Where was Lilbert, anyway?" someone asked. Moments later someone else voiced the same question. It certainly did not seem that far when we were on the bus.

We did not think it was possible for a whole community to just up and move, but Lilbert had done that very thing. Must have. The five of us considered amongst ourselves what might have happened. "Who could have moved Lilbert?" We queried each other. Suddenly, we knew.

Aliens! Yes. It was aliens all right. Martians had overheard us planning our trip to Lilbert and with malice aforethought they had moved the town.

We realized that the heat was getting to us, but we were also convinced that Lilbert had been moved. Having never walked the distance before we had no idea how long it should take to travel four miles. Still-and-all though, Lilbert had been moved. We were convinced.

We did not attempt to theorize a motive for the martians moving Lilbert. Motives were unimportant. What mattered was that the town had been moved, increasing the distance we had to walk by at least fifty miles.

The sound of the approaching truck grew louder. At this point we were certain it was a truck because of the heavy-sounding engine. Either that, or someone was having a serious mechanical problem with their car.

There it was. Why, it was Aunt Jeffie. We recognized her '64 navy blue Chevy pickup while it was hundreds of feet away, and boy, were we glad to see it.

We were so tired by then that we would most assuredly have given up any notion of completing the trip for pride's sake and gladly jumped into the back of the truck for a lift. If she had stopped. Apparently that was not the plan. Oh, it was our plan all right, but it most certainly was not Aunt Jeffie's.

Aunt Jeffie bore down on us like a bat out of hell. She drew up even with us and passed us all in the same instant, not even glancing our way.

Zoom! She swooshed by. We swayed in the draft her flying truck created. It would not have taken much to blow us on over. After regaining our balance we stood stock-still for long moments, our mouths hanging open and our tongues wagging, both from thirst and from disbelief that she would do that to us.

We were stunned, so much so that by unspoken agreement we ignored that this had even occurred and slowly trudged on as if nothing had happened!

It became increasingly hot, and we had not thought to bring so much as a drop of water. By now the sun was high in the sky. Our clothes were wet with sweat and our feet were raising blisters faster than corn popping in a hot skillet. We were all wearing plain sneakers. Plain and cheap. Our foot gear certainly did not help our situation.

Onward we trudged toward Lilbert. As we drew within sight of Robertson's Grocery we heard a truck door slam. We knew it was Aunt Jeffie and we figured she was about to leave the store. We hurried, deluding ourselves into thinking she would let us ride with her. As we reached the store Aunt Jeffie was cranking the truck. She saw us, we knew she did, but she pretended that she didn't. We were too out-done to yell at her to get her attention so we watched, mute as statues, as she put the truck in gear and pulled away. We stood back, well out of her way, and let her drive on by us. We were dumbfounded and confused by her treatment of us. And we were exhausted.

With our tongues nearly dragging the ground and our clothes wringing wet with sweat we pushed our way into the store. We bought ice cream cones and a couple of sodas. We only had enough money for two cans of pop, so the five of us shared them. We were dehydrated and thirsty but two cans of pop was all we got. It would have to do.

Thus fortified we began the four mile trek home. Finally, we were energetic enough and angry enough to vent our wrath at Aunt Jeffie. She would never know about it, of course, but we hurled all manner of insults at her quickly disappearing navy blue truck.

How dare she drive right by us, like we were ghosts. (We had begun to feel that we soon would be, but we hadn't been when she passed us.) We were mad! We knew it did us no good to get angry— we were still walking—but it did make us feel a little better to spew forth the venomous thoughts which threatened to choke us.

The ice cream and two sodas went a long way toward refreshing us. We would make it, we thought. We held that optimism for about a minute before doubts assailed us once again. And once again we ragged out Aunt Jeffie for leaving us.

We walked on with no play and very little conversation. We just walked, barely managing to put one poorly-shod foot in front of the other. We were so hot, *so* tired. Finally, we were forced to admit the heretofore unmentionable: we were going to die out there on that lonely road.

We figured it would take Aunt LA, the last relative we had spoken with, approximately two weeks to notice that she had not seen her nieces for a while. It would take her another week to remember to tell somebody. A month or so later someone might rouse himself to come looking for us. By then it would be much

Sitting, Uncle Luther, Aunt LA, and Uncle Claude; Standing, Aunt Jeffie and Uncle Walter

too late, our bones would be bleached and disjointed, scattered all over East Texas by ravenous vultures and armadillos.

Aunt Jeffie would be the lone possessor of the truth, fully knowledgeable of the cause of our deaths. Naturally, she would never tell anyone. Since there were so many victims, and young ones at that, she probably would have gotten the chair for indirectly causing our demise, so it would be in her best interest never to admit what she knew.

With visions of hungry buzzards circling overhead we plodded on, newly motivated by the thought of legions of carrion plucking our tender entrails.

Two miles down the road we neared Black Jack cemetery. This meant little to us as far as it being a cemetery. There were no black folks in it. Actually, there were no folks in it of any kind, only bones, coffins, and headstones. The cemetery was named "Black Jack" for some other reason having nothing to do with the color or race of its inhabitants. What was significant about the cemetery was that nearby sat a wondrous vision, a navy blue Chevrolet pickup. Aunt Jeffie had mercy upon us. Either that or she was having mechanical trouble in the worst way. No sane person would sit by anybody's (no pun intended) cemetery if they could help it.

It appeared that Aunt Jeffie was indeed waiting for us. We did not trust it at first. We thought she would torment us further by driving off as we approached the truck.

We eased up to the Chevy fully expecting that at any second she would start up, throw that truck in gear, and leave us in the dust. She did do this, but only one time before allowing us to jump on. She just had to have one more laugh at our expense. Through her side-mounted rearview mirror we saw Aunt Jeffie grinning as she spun off from us that first time. For about fifty yards she drove as if on a race track. Then she braked abruptly, pitched the truck into reverse and backed up. She backed up as swiftly as she had gone forward. A truly frightening sight to behold.

We jumped out of the way of the quickly approaching truck. It was then that the thought occurred to us. We were not dying fast enough for Aunt Jeffie. She was going to speed up the action by running us down!

We were smarter the next time Aunt Jeffie stopped. We stood back for a while, exercising extreme caution as we finally approached. This lady was armed and dangerous, after all. She had a truck and a license to use it! We knew, though, that if we ever got inside that truck bed there was no way she would be able to drag us out. The problem was getting to the truck before she jetted off.

On unspoken cue, we rushed the truck. All at once the five of us sprinted the thirty or so feet and jumped onto the tailgate before Aunt Jeffie had time to even release the clutch. After we were settled safely in the truck's bed Aunt Jeffie engaged the transmission and drove off. We could hear her in the cab, roaring with laughter, her head bobbing up and down with great, huge bursts of hysterical chortles.

We looked at each other, confused. Then it dawned on us. She had not planned to dust us that second time at all. We had run for nothing and used up energy we could ill afford to waste. Aunt Jeffie had gotten us again, making us run like wild horses to catch a truck that wasn't going anywhere without us.

By tacit agreement, we never spoke about our humiliation, instead choosing to ignore the shame that went along with it. We were not embarrassed by what Aunt Jeffie had done do us. We were embarrassed by being unable to walk the full eight miles and thus causing ourselves to be victims of Aunt Jeffie's humor.

If Aunt Jeffie had not happened along I imagine we would have lain down in that shady "white folks" cemetery and died. Dead folks don't care what race their neighbors are. Be that as it may, we were elated to be rescued and glad to avoid the tragedy of five girls dying from heat exhaustion while walking home from the ice cream store. What an irony that would have been.

We never tried it again. To this day!

I can walk eight miles now with ease. But I never walk to Lilbert. Both stores closed years ago. One burned down and the other is now a storage building. There would be no ice cream cone for my troubles, and my friends would not be with me. What would be the point?

CHAPTER 4: CHURCH ESTABLISHMENTS

County Line Baptist Church was established in the 1890s. It began as a modest frame structure. It was located just above the bend in the road on the north side of Aunt LA's home. Rumor had it that the original burned to the ground when a visiting neighbor started a big fire in the wood heater. The fire became much bigger than he ever intended.

Anyway, after this building burned, a new church was constructed about a hundred yards away. It was on the same road but closer to the middle of the community, just across from Uncle Claude's store. It, too, was a modest frame building, considerably less modest than the original one. The second structure is the church my generation grew up a part of. This is also where many of the community's residents were bade farewell as they lay stretched before the pulpit. Years ago the church was remodeled. The choir loft and pulpit were relocated from the side of the church to the front. This is a more conventional arrangement, but I miss the right-side placement of the loft and pulpit.

The memories held within those walls bespeak of an era when the church was the center of the community, when everyone

County Line Baptist Church, 1990

Sister Ruth and the County Line Baptist Church Choir perform during Homecoming service

and almost everything was rooted in religion. Sunday morning brought with it the assurance that we would attend Sunday school and church. There was no discussion on the matter. It was not an option. Unless we were sick—very sick—we attended church.

In our younger years Big Sister, Sister Girl, Jeffie Mae, Chee-Chee, and I were an integral part of the choir. Our voices were young and strong, though largely untalented. We had a wonderful time singing in the choir, especially since by some quirk we all managed to sit in the rear section. The women reigned in the forward pews of the choir loft, just behind the preachers' chairs.

During boring sermons we girls whispered to each other and passed notes. We chewed gum and ate candy. All this was fine and good as long as we did not get caught. Ingenious strategies were devised to ensure that this did not happen. We covered our giggles with strangled coughs. We chewed gum and blew bubbles behind our hand fans, and we made sure that we did more note passing than whispering. Whispering was simply too dangerous in spite of our caution. These schemes must have been effective because

Homecoming Opening

none of us was ever knocked off the bench by any of the sisters sitting in front. That would have been our fate had our shenanigans been discovered. Our activities certainly made those dry "fire and brimstone" sermons easier to ignore.

The days passed swiftly from the time school dismissed in May until the first big event of the summer. The All-Night Singing was held on the second Saturday night in July. It is an annual event, which for school-aged children signals the mid-point of summer vacation.

For the occasion, neighbors and local church members were invited to spend the evening with our church family, singing and praising the Lord. Sometimes the singing went on until well after midnight, thus the title of the event. This was a time of great excitement for us kids. There was not a lot else to do, and we could only spend so much time hanging out at the store. Going to church was a great social occasion.

July's All-Night Singing and the Annual Homecoming in August were by far the biggest and most important events in the area. Everybody in the community turned out, Uncle Claude included. Even though he lived and worked just across the road from the church, Uncle Claude always drove the short distance. It seemed to me that, although he used crutches, it would have been simpler just to walk across. I never saw him do that, though. He walked the short distance to his truck, threw his sticks in the back, climbed in and took off.

The International was always parked "heading into the driveway." There was a large sycamore tree directly in front of the parking space, necessitating backwards maneuvering. Uncle Claude had backed that truck out of his driveway so many times that he never—and I mean never—looked back to see what was behind him. He never hit anything, either. Everyone knew not to block Uncle Claude's driveway, so there was nothing behind him except his own building. He made the short trip for decades with nary a mishap. Once on the church campus Uncle Claude parked in his usual spot and walked into the church, managing the five steep concrete steps with little difficulty.

The All-Night Singing was the only event of the year that required the church campus to be rigged with extra lighting. The bare 100-watt bulbs were strung about the churchyard, hanging perilously from electrical lines which had been attached to trees and poles. The bulbs provided ample light for the outside area. They also attracted lots of bugs. There were bugs inside the church as well since the open windows were screen-less, but not nearly as many as there were outside.

The extra outdoor lighting illuminated the entire campus but was especially handy in the area near and around the soda-water stand. This stand was a simple wooden affair built years before specifically for the purpose of dispensing soft drinks. 1 × 12 pine planks were nailed to posts and convenient trees, forming a square, box-like structure.

There was a ledge of the same material on one side of the stand. The ledge served as a counter over which the soda and money changed from one hand to the other. Inside the stand were several large #3 galvanized wash tubs filled with ice and soda. Underneath the counter was an old cigar box used to hold the proceeds from the soda sale. That was all we sold at the stand, though you could buy barbeque sandwiches over at the mobile pit. The pit was parked nearer to the road, a bit away from the church to keep annoying smoke away. Throughout the evening people chatted while roaming the church yard, punctuating their time outside with visits to the soda stand and the barbeque pit.

Church services were being conducted, so no one stayed outside for more than a few minutes at a time. For the duration of the service there were constant streams of folks coming and going. We kids enjoyed being outside but we dared not remain long. It was extremely embarrassing to have our mother or other adult come outside to get us. That did not happen often. Most of the time the adults were so engrossed in the service that they did not notice our absence. Then again, once was enough.

After a group sang their selections they meandered outside for fresh air and a cold drink. It got mighty hot in that old un-air-conditioned church, and the only way to cool off was to step outside. Singers, individuals and groups strolled outside the sanctuary. They mopped their brows with already sopping handkerchiefs in an attempt to find a modicum of relief from the stifling heat.

We did not mind the heat; the excitement of the service more than offset the discomfort we endured. These were high times in County Line. Next to the store, the church was our favorite place to be. Admittedly, our religious experience was not what it should have been because we were so very intent upon having a good time. We did have fun at church, albeit surreptitiously.

The singings were rich fodder for our active imaginations. Oftentimes the people who sang were sources of amusement themselves. It was not that the singers lacked talent. Many were quite good, but they tended to get so involved with their singing that they carried on and on. Sometimes one song lasted over ten minutes. We found this both ridiculous and hilarious.

For weeks after the program one of us would occasionally burst out in song. Our renditions elicited riotous laughter as we emulated the singers. Nothing was sacred. We even went so far as to mimic the high, keening falsetto voices of what were supposed to be tenors.

"EEEEEEEEEEEEEE," we sang, in a reasonable imitation of the hair-raising notes. We pranced around on our "stage," moving agilely in time to the music we made ourselves. Empty soda bottles were our microphones and our audience was anything or anybody unfortunate enough to be near—dogs, cats, siblings. We enthusiastically encouraged each other in our foolishness.

"Come on up. Come on up!" someone shouted, sounding for all the world like Mr. Jessie Morrisette. Another shook and shuddered before pretending to fall away in a dead faint, ostensibly overcome by the almighty power of the Holy Spirit. The faintee was very careful about where she fell. No sense in getting too carried away.

It is a wonder and a testament to His grace that God did not strike us dead.

In actuality, many folks who heard that kind of high-pitched screaming—oops! "singing"—really enjoyed it. Oh how they shouted, encouraging the entertainers to keep going, sustaining their efforts to lift their voices higher and higher. Mr. Jessie Morrisette was certainly one so inclined, and he rarely missed an opportunity to listen to those soulful renditions of the gospel. Without fail, Mr. Morrisette claimed his favorite spot. Whatever the occasion, whether an All-Night Singing or just regular church service, he was always there—right in front of the pulpit.

Mr. Morrisette was an extremely thin man, a long narrow mass of tightly bonded skin and bone—skin and bone, with little in between. His head was small and bony and was covered with a thin crown of wavy black hair. His high prominent cheekbones suggested Indian ancestry. When he smiled, Mr. Morrisette's ill-fitting false teeth and his emaciated countenance made him resemble a skeleton with its protuberant jaw stretched in a permanent grin.

Unwary preachers, perhaps visiting for the first time, must have been unsettled to look down from the pulpit into the visage of Mr. Morrisette. Seeing him for the first time had to be a bit disconcerting. The sight of a live skeleton grinning and shouting "Come on up!" could have caused the less devout to do the same: come on up and out of the church as fast as their feet could speed them away. Skeletons belong in the cemetery. They have already had their time in church.

Mr. Morrisette enjoyed good singing and good preaching. When the singers or preachers were deeply enthralled with their craft, others were incited to shout and "get happy." Mr. Morrisette jumped up from his seat on the front bench. He waved his handkerchief and yelled out, "Come on up! Come on up!"

Sometimes he took a few steps toward the performers as if he intended to join them in their singing or preaching. "Come on up! Come on up!" he demanded.

Where was "up"? Well, I suppose it was the higher plane of spiritual actualization.

Mr. Morrisette was certainly not the only one who got involved in church service. Aunt Louisiana also had a ritual. It is impossible to adequately describe what her ritual was, but it was far less physical than Mr. Morrisette's routine.

Aunt LA demonstrated her excitement about her church experience by softly singing dirges. Her elegies were chant-like—melodious in form, but with few words. "Lead me on, my father," she softly entreated, with a pathos born of the intimate knowledge of suffering. Sometimes she added, "Well, well, well, my father." Often she just moaned, repeating these invocations throughout the service, her voice soothing and gentle.

The singing sometimes sounded melancholy and sorrowful, but Aunt LA was not sad—she was just "caught up" with the burden of praying for the lost. We knew that was what she did even though we rarely heard the words she used. It was not important that we understood, for she was not speaking to us.

Aunt LA was a dear old soul, prayerful and devout. She also had a very dry sense of humor. One had to be quick to dodge the consequence of her jocularity. Aunt LA teased us frequently, but one time she really got off with Byrd.

When I was about twelve years old, my older sister Marceline (Byrd) and her family unfortunately lost their home and most of their belongings in a fire. Naturally, everyone in the community pitched in to help them replace some of their things, Aunt LA included.

It was the early Seventies and Auntie was an established octogenarian, well over eighty years old. The old gal was still sharp mentally and had a powerful grip as well. When her nieces, nephews, or grandkids came to visit her, she patted and squeezed arms and legs the whole time. I thought then she did this to see how fat we were. No matter our girth, Aunt LA continually encouraged us to share food with her whenever we dropped by.

With the wisdom brought by passing years, I now understand that the squeezes and the food were her ways of demonstrating her considerable affection. The family in general was relatively un-demonstrative when it came to showing love. Aunt LA's squeezes were really mini-hugs on the sly.

Anyway, one Sunday afternoon Byrd stopped by Aunt LA's house on her way to her home. Auntie's house was the last one in the community that set near the road, and so hers was the last visible home on the way out of the community. Byrd had attended church that morning and decided to visit her aunt before heading home.

Auntie was a bit on the frail side and stayed home much of the time. She had not been in church that day, preferring to stay home wrapped up in her lap robe. Visitors were always welcome, but Aunt LA was particularly fond of her niece Byrd.

Byrd tapped softly on the wooden front door. She stood at the door a few moments and then, as was the local custom, walked into the living room without waiting for a response. No one locked their doors back then and, as long as the visitor identified himself as he hopped upon the porch, it was perfectly acceptable to just walk on in.

Aunt LA sang out a hello in response to Byrd's jolly greeting.

"Come on in, Byrd," her strong voice rang out. Byrd walked into the kitchen where Aunt LA sat warming by the stove. The two exchanged pleasantries for a few minutes. Byrd asked after Auntie's health, specifically inquiring about the rheumatism that plagued her.

Auntie asked how the church service had been that morning and so forth. She was genuinely interested in the topic and content of the morning's sermon. Byrd did not remember much but somehow managed to rattle off an acceptable synopsis.

After being in her home for a few minutes, Byrd began to do what she invariably did whenever she visited, taking down and re-braiding her aunt's hair. As she stood behind her carefully combing Auntie's thin white strands, Byrd's mind naturally began to wander, snapping to attention only when she realized she was being addressed.

"Byrd?" Auntie softly called.

"Ma'am?" Byrd answered, respectful as always.

"Did I give you anything when your house burned down?" Auntie asked with a sense of seemingly genuine puzzlement.

Byrd, sensitive to Auntie's age and probable memory failure, began to detail the items Auntie had in fact given her. "Yessum, you did. You gave me some white bath towels and a bathroom rug and a skillet and some cooking utensils." Byrd paused to collect her thoughts. "Oh yeah," she continued, "you gave me a sauce pan and some peaches." (Auntie had canned the peaches herself.)

Auntie was silent a moment. "Byrd," she finally said.

Byrd continued her combing, parting and braiding Auntie's air as she worked her way from top to back. "Yessum," she answered. My poor sister could not imagine what was coming next. She figured LA would ask her if there was anything else she needed for her house or her kids. She would, of course, decline any such offer.

"You bring some of my things back here," Auntie said, her face as straight as an iron poker. "You know I didn't mean to give you all that." She turned to look at Byrd, fully aware that her favorite niece had no idea she was teasing.

To her credit Byrd was flabbergasted for only a split second— just long enough for her to realize that she had been "gotten off with." By the time Byrd realized that she was being teased, Aunt LA was almost doubled over in laughter, unable to contain her mirth.

Aunt LA had not the slightest intention of making Byrd bring anything back. It would never have occurred to her to even consider such a thing. I believe she simply wanted to lighten up a bad situation.

Well, Auntie and Byrd laughed for a good long while. Byrd never forgot the story; it is still one of her favorites. I believe it continues to vex her that she was so taken in by our aunt and that she was never able to outdo that practical joke.

Score one for LA.

Marceline (Byrd) in
high school

That Byrd loved Aunt LA deeply is evidenced by the fact that when she died back in 1974, Byrd stayed right there in her hospital room with her body until the attendants came to take Auntie to the funeral home. Byrd is powerfully scared of ghosts and haunts and such. She would never have sat up with just any other deceased relative, and she admitted as much. This was someone so special to Byrd that she later claimed to have not been frightened in the least. She's not done such a thing since, and she is still acutely afraid of ghosts.

As I think back, I realize that getting prepared to go to church was a cultural undertaking in and of itself. We were a long way from wealthy so we had to "make do." These days most of us would hesitate to admit some of the things we "made do" with back then, let alone try them. Someone on Oprah's show just the other day mentioned eating Vick's salve for colds. They said you should not do it, but if the stuff was bad for you, we would all be dead. It was all part of our local culture.

For breakfast on Sundays Mama usually fried a big batch of chicken. This was served with homemade biscuits, rice, and gravy. We ate like hogs before getting dressed. Mama always made the Sunday dessert on Saturday afternoon, often baking a cake in her huge, stainless steel roasting pan. Mama would prepare the rest of Sunday dinner as she made breakfast. The meal was reheated when we returned from church.

After breakfast we began getting ready for church. We pressed our clothes the day before. Mama did not allow us to iron on Sunday, but for some inexplicable reason it was fine to polish shoes on Sunday. Our black patent-leather Sunday shoes were shiny due to their factory finish. Patent leather is always shiny, but to really gloss them we used a biscuit leftover from breakfast. We took a cold biscuit and briskly rubbed it into the leather. The shortening in the biscuits made the shoes really glisten. The only problem was that if we walked to church, the shortening also attracted the red sandy dust to our shoes. We solved this by always carrying a rag with us. Once we got inside the church we whipped out the rag and dusted our shoes off, refreshing that wonderful shine.

A funny thing about those biscuits: if they were particularly tasty, our shoes oddly didn't need much shining. If the biscuits weren't that great, it was, "Boy, are my shoes dull!" That took care of the rest of the biscuits and saved us from having to eat them.

Our shoes were not the only things shining—our legs and faces were as well. We achieved this shine by smearing them with small amounts of tallow. Tallow is rendered pork fat. No wonder the dogs were always following us.

Sunday school started promptly at 9:45. There were separate classes for the adults (them) and the children (us). Cousin Puff taught the children's class for several years while she lived in the community.

Uncle N. E.'s youngest daughter, Anita (Puff), grew up in County Line but had married and moved away. She came back to be near her parents while her husband did duty in Korea. After he came home they moved away again. From that point on, we either taught ourselves or joined in with the adult class.

As time wore on, we young 'uns became a more integral part of the adult classes. One of us often served as Sunday school secretary. We wrote and read the minutes or Sunday school report. It was an honor. The church minutes have hardly changed through the years. Minutes and Sunday school reports—a record of each Sunday school session—are still hand written, either in a ledger or a regular school-style spiral notebook. *Our* minutes tended to be long and wordy documents written to showcase our writing talent. Once we took over the duties of keeping them we never abbreviated or wrote anything other than grammatically and politically correct statements. No "moved in second" for us. "Moved in second" is a corruption of the parliamentary term "moved and seconded." It is sometimes seen in earlier church minutes because of either ignorance or tradition, or perhaps it was written by the "traditionally ignorant."

At this time the church secretary is Sis. Claudia Maye Joyce (formerly Claudia Maye Ross). The treasurer is Sis. Gertie Lee Ruffin. Deacon Monel Upshaw still serves as Sunday School Superintendent, after about a hundred years in the position. Sis. Ruffin's husband Willie Ray (B) is the Assistant Superintendent. The superintendents use the little chrome and black dinner bell to dismiss classes and to bring meetings to order. The bell has been in service longer than I can say. It is one of the few original icons of past church history remaining.

The church has been remodeled and re-outfitted. The old homemade pulpit is gone and the homemade benches were given away or stored. Standing in their stead is a traditional pulpit finely crafted of lustrous solid maple. The new pews are equally luxuriant, with solid foam, built-in cushions and color-coordinated covers. The church has central heat and air now, so the cardboard hand fans are seldom used. Carpet and new sub-flooring replaced the three-inch pine planks of yesteryear. Before the remodel, there

County Line Baptist Church, 2009

were several places in the floor where the pine knots had fallen away; you could see the ground beneath the church. No more!

It's much different now. I admit that I don't really miss going "down" to the ladies' restroom. This was a rather fancy outhouse, but an outhouse nonetheless.

No, the things I miss aren't things at all: I miss the people who were the church's foundation. Although the sub-flooring may turn to 3/4 inch plywood and the three-inch pine planks may turn into blue dense cut-pile carpet with stain resistance, there will never come a time when the true foundation of the church will be remodeled. It will always be what it always was and the memories will always be held within those hallowed walls.

The fact that our ancestors were able to establish and build a church fresh out of slavery and that we are able to maintain and improve it is a tribute to them, not to us. We are what we are because of what they were made of. One of the reasons these few scribbles were set down was so that we never forget.

CHAPTER 5: THE CHURCH MINUTES: HOME MISSIONARY SOCIETY

(H.M.S., no, this is not "Her Majesty's Ship")

These are samples of church minutes from 1940–44 for your reading pleasure. They will make more sense if you are already familiar with our family tree. I have taken the liberty of correcting spelling and grammar only to the extent necessary to make these entries readable, not wanting to distort their charming character. These earlier examples *are* grammatically and politically incorrect. Fixing them was more than I could bear and would have totally negated the point of including them in the first place.

"What is the point in including these entries?" you may well ask. The answer lies in the making of a community, the changes and similarities of an ongoing culture; they embody our past and betoken what is important to us.

The Church Minutes vindicate the old adage, "The more things change, the more they remain the same."

Following each section is a brief explanation with corrections as needed. Minor corrections are in parentheses and italicized beside the error.

Sept 13, 1940
Opening . . . *(song?)*, "I have a robe." Scripture reading by the president. Hymn, "Guide Me Over" by Sis. Bailey. Prayer led by Juanita Tinsley.

Sis. Beatrice Bailey	10 cents
Sis. Lorine Ross	10
Sis. Wallace	5
Sis. Mary Ross	10
Sis. Juanita Tinsley	10

Been both moved and seconded that Sis. Beatrice Bailey elected delegate, motion carried.

It has been both moved in second that Sis. Juanita Tinsley issure *(issue)* out envelope fore *(for)* the society.

Been both moved in second that the society adjourn until fourth Sunday in Sept.

Closing song by Sis. Lorine Ross "Till we meet again."

President Sis. Wallace

Secretary Sis. Juanita Tinsley

These were minutes from Sunday school; they detail the attendees' donations as well as what songs were sung. "Guide Me Over" should have been written "Guide Me O Thou Great Jehovah."

It was moved and seconded that Sister Beatrice Bailey serve as the delegate to the Missionary Baptist Association *(meeting)*.

"Been both moved in second. . . ." Should read "been moved and seconded. . . ."

Sept. 20, 1936

The County Line H.M.S. was called to order by the pres. read four *(for)* verses of the 26 chapter of Matthew. Hymn title "My Soul be on Thy Guard" after witch *(which "witch" I don't know; perhaps the word is simply "which.")*

Prayer by Sis. Lorine Erving. Song "Get Right With God."

Motion in second we take up unfinish business *(moved and seconded that we take up unfinished. . . .)* Some timely remarks was made by the sisters. Motion that we take up new business *(moved that we take. . . .)*

Motion that we stand a join *(adjourned)* until Tues. Night.

Closing song "Get Right with God."

Dismiss *(dismissed)* by the Reverend

Pres. Sis. Upshaw

Sec. Sis. Mary Ross

Sis. Mattie Erving

Sis. Juanita Tinsley

February 7, 1943

The County Line H.M.S. opened about 1:30. Opening song "When the Saints go Marching in," prayer by Sis. Lar *(Laura)* Upshaw, Jr.*

Paying of dues.	Sis. L.A. Wallace	5 cents
	Sis. Laura Upshaw	
	(Big Laura)	5
	Sis. Jeffie Ross	5
	Sis. Mars Session	5

(I wonder if this was Venus's sister)

By common concent *(consent)* we heard the report of the delegate. The report was nice. She purchased a guide and a plaid card *(?)*. Motion and second*(ed)* that the report of the delegate be received. Motion met with a second that we take up new business. Motion carried. Some suggestions were made on plan to raise money for the painting of the church, motion carried.

Motion and second*(ed)* that we have an entainment *(entertainment)* on the third Saturday. *(Apparently, there was then some discussion about what everyone was going to bring)*

Sis. L.A. Wallace—cake, poly-pop

Sis. Viola Upshaw—cake, poly-pop, sugar

Sis. Beatrice Bailey—two pies

Sis. Mary Session—cake

Sis. Laura Upshaw—chicken

Sis. T.S.—chicken *(unsure if she was bringing chicken or if "chicken" was her last name)*

Deacon Tinsley—3 loafs *(loaves)* of bread

Rev. Bailey—money.

Motion and seconded that madams *(Mesdames; surely they didn't really mean the word in this spelling . . . as in madams—ladies of the night.)* Lula Mae Erving, Ruth Hazel

Ross, Murlee *(Myrtle Lee?)* Upshaw, Earnestean Tinsley, Mrs. Hooper, and Mrs. Blakey assist the girls in getting up a program for the third Saturday night.

Report of the districe *(district)* board by Sis. L.A. Wallace. Reports a nice time *(was had by all?).* Motion met with a second *(Isn't a "second" the person who stands with you during a duel? Well, not right with you, but watches your back, so to speak)* that we adjourn until the fourth Saturday evening.

Pres. Sis. L.A. Wallace

Sec. T.S. Whitaker

*[Junior because this Laura was married to Jim Upshaw, Jr., also known as "Little Jim." Jim's mother was also named Laura, so Big Jim's wife became known as "Big Laura" or "Laura, Sr." and Little Jim's wife was known as "Little Laura" or "Laura, Jr." But then, if you've read this far you probably already figured that out.]

I added these minutes to the book because they open the door for me to speak now about our present church community. One thing that hasn't changed very much is the style of the church minutes.

CHAPTER 6: HOLINESS CHURCH

Not all of our "church" memories were of the Baptist church in the community, though for years that was the only one (church) we had. A number of years ago, when my set (Chee-Chee, Sister Girl, Jeffie Mae, Big Sister) were young teenagers, a new denomination came to town.

Elder and Sister Moore scouted County Line and decided that what the community needed was a "holiness" church. They started out having services in the old school house. This is the one-story building which shares the campus with the church—the Baptist church, that is. The building had been largely unused for ages. Classes had been suspended there some twenty years earlier.

As a child I visited the building many times just to look around, basking in the glow of the school's former glory. I played "dress up" with the paper dresses that had been stored there. I have no idea who or why anyone wore paper clothing, but I recollect those dresses were rather festive in style and design. A bright yellow ruffled number with a very full skirt caught my eye time and time again. It was my favorite costume and I never stopped wondering who may have worn it back in the "glory days." I have often been reminded of that dress and never stopped wondering who may have worn it.

There wasn't much else of interest in the old school. The architecture was plain and simple, the floors and walls crafted of pine planking. There was an elevated area at the north end of the building called the "stage." The platform was about two feet higher than the main floor and ran the entire length of the room.

When the Moores decided to have church there, they already had a neighbor. Cousin Harold lived in the rooms comprising the other side of the building, and was an unwilling audience to the services next door. He never said anything about what he heard, but I know it was a lot.

The Moores started out having church just about every night, but downshifted to three times weekly. At first, just about

Terence Dennis, grandson of Monel and Leota, in front of the old County Line school house

everybody in the community came to church. That soon dwindled down, too. The steadies were Mama Odie, Cousin Venora and her daughters Cathey Mae and Velma Lee, Aunt Jeffie and her girls Big Sister, Jeffie Mae, and Chee-Chee, Sister Girl and me. There was also a group that came from Nacogdoches with the Moores. Most nights there were about 15–20 saints in service. Actually, we were not all considered "saints." You only got to be a "saint" when Elder Moore said you were "saved." I guess God was busy.

I never did make it. Neither did Chee-Chee or Jeffie Mae. Velma Lee, Cathey Mae and Sister Girl got "saved and sanctified," even living impressibly holy lives for a while. The girls eventually traded holiness for fun, though, unfortunately losing their sanctification in the process.

I suppose the older women got saved, too, I just don't recall. I do recall the long hours in testimony service, listening to the same testimonies again and again. This was kind of a drag, but the real drag was the prayer time. We girls spent literally hundreds of hours "seeking" the Holy Ghost. It would be years before I discovered that the Holy Ghost never had been lost. Back then, though, we believed it when they said we had to spend hours on our knees on the hard wooden floor, making them rustier and rustier.

Praises to Allah for true enlightenment!

Night after night and Sunday after Sunday we sought the Lord. We spent so much time on our knees that it's not hard to figure out why we soon reached the point of nonchalance. School and rest were more important to us; we still had to get up early in the mornings no matter how late we were up "seeking."

Our collective id soon began to figure out ways to discreetly catnap during services. This wasn't easy. The benches were hard; the building was always either stiflingly hot in summer or unbearably cold in winter, with icy blasts of North wind rushing in through the cracks in the walls and floors. With that discomfort, sleep was often elusive. We did our best, though, quickly learning that the best opportunity to sleep was during the "seeking" part of the service. The elevated stage was our "moaners" bench, our praying place. If you positioned yourself just right you could manage to appear pious and in deep prayer while snoring quietly at the same time. You had to be a light sleeper, though, because when it came time to rise up from your rusty knees you couldn't lag. That is how Jeffie Mae got caught sleeping one night.

We had been at church for several hours and had reached the point in the service where we did as described above. We all flocked to the altar for prayer. We teenagers kind of looked forward to this because, of course, we got to catch some zzzzzz's. On this particular occasion, the building was actually quite cozy—neither too hot nor too cold. Someone had built up a big fire in the old wood stove several hours before church started, driving out the bitter chill.

All that warmth was bound to have an effect on us. Sure enough, before Elder Moore could even reach his first "hallelujah" we were nodding, our heads moving up and down, not in agreement, but in sleep.

One of us, namely Jeffie Mae, was engaged in more of the head nodding suggestive of light slumber. This child was enjoying deep, serious, REM-class sleep. That was fine as long as you could still hear and thus know when it was time to end your nap. Poor Jeffie Mae was too far gone to hear anything except the sound of sheep nimbly leaping over fences.

Elder Moore prayed on and on. We slept. He prayed some more, we slept some more. He finally ended his prayer, and we rose stiffly from our places, rusty knees creaking painfully as we hobbled to our seats. Jeffie Mae slept on, snoring softly. The church was quiet now as we waited for testimony to begin. Jeffie Mae's snoring sounded like a chorus of diesel engines; everyone knew she was deeply involved in what she was doing—sleeping.

The rest of us sat down on the edge of the stage in preparation for the final section of the service: testimony. Those of us on either side of her tried to wake her, surreptitiously nudging her feet and hunching her shoulders. I guess Jeffie Mae was really tired because she simply could not be roused. Aunt Jeffie was furiously angry by now, and getting angrier by the minute. She reached over none-too-gently and snatched her granddaughter up by the scruff of her neck. "Get up from there, Jeffie Mae," she hissed.

You can imagine!

Jeffie Mae jumped up like a thoroughbred shooting from his stall, instantly alert—and ready to testify. Perhaps she did have an interesting dream; she couldn't have been planning to testify about anything else. We still tease her about this, but I suspect this is one of those memories she would just as soon forget.

There are a number of other memories from that era which elicit smiles, even today many years later. There was the time my Cousin Leonia decided to grace our church with her unaccompanied and unaccomplished voice. We were at the sanctified church as usual one Tuesday evening. I had gotten really tired and sleepy and had retired to my father's pickup truck parked just in front of the building. Usually, Mama did not allow us to leave church for any reason. Looking back, I realize I must have told her I was sick or something. In any case, I was asleep in the truck rather than inside the church when the big event occurred.

I was deep in my slumber when I was awakened by the din of the local dogs. The "church dogs," as we called them, were community mongrels that for some reason liked to hang out around the holiness church whenever we were in service. This night was no exception. The mongrels were in full attendance. What was unusual was the fact that the dogs were howling ferociously, waking me with their long, piteous howls. I rose up off the seat, fully alert. *What could cause the mutts to go on like that*, I wondered.

I was puzzled for but a few seconds. Moments after the animals had awakened me with their howling, I heard piteous howling of another sort. Human howling. "What in the world?" I could not believe my ears. Cousin Leonia was "singing." The song was something about a train being at the station and how sinners were admonished to "get on board." After she "sang" this line she began to make a noise which I am sure she thought was akin to a train whistle.

"Whooooooo, whoooooo," she went, on and on. Every time she "whistled" the dogs would howl, offering up their own rendition. I was never sure if the dogs knew they were supposed to sound like train whistles, or if they were simply trying to sound like Cousin Leonia. There is also the possibility that the dogs were howling in protest. I found out later that the folks unlucky enough to be inside the church were just as dismayed as I was. They couldn't believe it, either. Cousin Leonia never sang—certainly not solos. Now we knew why! Those on the inside could hear the dogs' plaintive wailing from inside the church as easily as I could hear my cousin's moans from my perch in the truck. We laughed about that scene for years, although I truly hope Cousin Leonia never knew.

CHAPTER 7: LOUISIANA, ALABAMA: CHURCH ROOTS

It could be said that every single black person in America has roots in the South. The rich black, red, beige or multicolored dirt that grew such large bolls of cotton also fostered the growth of thousands of families now speckling the country. If you live in New York, your grandmother was from Alabama or perhaps North/South Carolina; if you live in California, dear old Granny was from Texas or Louisiana. There are those few misguided African Americans who honestly believe that all their ancestors were born and raised in New Jersey. Well, my response is, "They may have been born and raised there, but they most certainly were not bred there." Now, I do realize that that statement is in rather poor taste, so I will counter it by remarking on the wonderful way so many of us have assimilated ourselves into our culture. We'll leave it there.

It could also be said that every Black person in America has roots in the church. For some of us those roots extend way down, to China, maybe. Others have roots, but they are so shallow they are visible after a hard storm (of the literal and figurative variety). In any case, the roots are there. The church has been the most powerful force for the union of our people. It's common knowledge (if you aren't in the know about what I am about to comment on please don't tell anyone) that many of those wonderfully religious, submissive, innocent old Negro spirituals our forebears sang in the cotton fields were actually messages to each other regarding escape plans. Did you really think "Go Down Moses" had anything to do with the Israelites, or that "Swing Low, Sweet Chariot" was about waiting to die? It ain't necessarily so. That's just what those wily ones wanted their masters and mistresses to believe. I don't think the white folks caught on until fairly recently, when it was far too late.

The point is, everything about and for blacks was and is rooted in the church, particularly the very rise from slavery.

As sacred and as honorable as the church is, as wonderful an institution as it is and has been, as holy and as revered as those fire-breathing, spit-slinging, chicken-eating preachers are, there are incidents and accidents which amuse nonetheless because they relate to the church. Yes, we are still amused, though we often make futile attempts to hide our snickers behind our cardboard hand fans. You know, the ones with the picture of the cute little girl on the front, dressed in her Sunday best, and the advertisement for the funeral home on the back. Talk about your study in contrasts! Make no mistake about it, though, there's a whole lot of laughing going on in churches across America. I personally believe it adds to the allure of religiosity.

I remember a story I heard just the other week about church. Maye said she was out visiting one of the more "high society" black churches in the area. I won't be so crass as to name it, but if you were there, or know anyone who was, you already know it anyway.

The story goes that someone had invited a special guest to this musical extravaganza. This guest was of a different chromatical persuasion. Should I just say he was white? In a sea of black faces I don't have to tell you, he stood out. Now let me interject.

The gentleman was very warmly received, I am sure, and I am reasonably certain no one except perhaps the very young and the very old (who can get away with anything) stared at him (much). I can also assure you that everyone except the party who invited him wondered who he was and what he was doing there. The only reason his host/ess didn't wonder is because s/he knew already. I digress.

It soon became obvious why the man was there. Well, maybe that statement is a bit too general. I rephrase: it soon became obvious what the man was there to do. Why he chose to do it there remains a mystery.

As the program progressed different choirs, chorales, choruses, soloists, etc. went forth to entertain. Then, as his name was called, this stranger stood and walked toward the baby grand. Even idiots realized he was there to play the piano. (I am not suggesting there were any idiots in the congregation, but if there had been any visiting idiots they too would have been wise in this case.)

The man sat at the piano, graceful and confident. Maye says it was a piece by Brahms. She was certain of this because she was sitting close enough to the piano to look over the man's shoulder as he spread all his music about (that's the only reason she knew). Besides, she reasoned, being intelligent and all (certainly no idiot), only classical music could have that many notes.

The man began to play. Beautifully, according to Maye. (Did I mention that along with being a renowned surgeon, Maye is also a great music critic? I thought not.) The congregation was quite appreciative, obviously all great music aficionados in the crowd. They had such beatific expressions on their faces, really enjoying it they were. There was even an occasional exclamation. They were not loud exclamations and shouts like we black folks normally do in response to good music. No, these were soft, quiet reverential exclamations of pleasure.

"Yes, yes," several good sisters called out as their tall hats bobbed up and down in agreement. Incidentally, "tall hats" are the black women of the South's version of "big hair." The good brothers over in the deacons' section added their comments. "Amen, amen, amen."

The man played on, blissfully oblivious to the magnanimous accolades being quietly heaped upon him. He played and played and played. No doubt he hit keys on that piano that had not been touched since the ivory was laid on them. I just know he did not use the sustain pedal (that's the one on the right) to keep time as many ordinary southern good sisters and brothers who play for the church tend to do.

The young man must have been highly complimented to have those dear souls try and "gospel-ize" or shall I say "baptize" (this was a Baptist church) his music. We commend his nameless self for the bravery he exhibited.

Let us move on. I did mention fire-breathing, spit-slinging preachers, didn't I? I'll make no further comment on their love of fried chicken. Y'all know.

Preachers don't really breathe fire, but they most certainly do spit. Sometimes when they preach they get so much spit on the microphone that I fear electrocution. You know how some of them like to yank the mike from its stand and put it right up next to their juicy, wet lips as they scream and whoop and holler. The more "into it" these preachers get the more they stomp their feet and whoop and holler and the juicier and wetter their lips get. I do wonder if anyone has ever gotten a "buzz" from the mike while doing that. I think it would be judicious if preachers who do this were to begin wearing rubber soled shoes. Perhaps, though, they are already hip to this.

I often wondered, too, how the good sisters who so boldly shout and dance and run up and down the aisles know exactly where to rare (rear) back and fall. Is it divine influence that places a deacon or other stout body handily in her path? I don't believe I have ever seen or heard tell of anybody actually injuring themselves in one of these swoons. It seems that the finer and more comely the sister is the faster she is caught, but the longer it takes to right her and return her to her seat. I just wondered.

My family and I grew up with the church as the center of our social beings. The main events of our often dreadfully dull lives were Christmas and homecoming.

Children play a video game during Homecoming

Church homecomings are as much a mainstay and as solid an institution as anything I can think of. Every historically black church in the South has homecomings. If they don't, it's only because all the members have had their homegoing. It is *the* big event. The preaching is always good. The food is great, too, but it's the socializing—ha, the socializing. That's what homecoming is all about. People from far and near, relatives you didn't even know you had, friends from the dark ages—everybody comes to homecoming. It is the occasion to be spiritually renewed, coinciding as it does in our church with the annual revival, and socially refreshed. It's why we starve ourselves for those last few desperate weeks before the event. Can't have everyone talking about how much weight you've gained. It's why we patch things up with our spouses, at least enough for appearances. Don't want folks trying to get in our business. I don't really know about that last part, but I do know about the diet stuff. I do it myself every year.

Still, I reckon I better lay off the preachers and church. There are others in the church whose behavior warrants comments.

CHAPTER 8: COUSIN GILLIS, PETE, AND COOKING

When we were growing up we had a cousin by the name of Rev. John Gillis Upshaw. He lived about a mile and half away, somewhat less of a distance if you took the shortcut through Uncle N. E.'s pasture. Cousin Gillis was a very well-known minister pastoring several churches in the general area. He was also a dignitary in the Missionary Baptist Convention, often serving as Moderator in the association.

As he grew older, Cousin Gillis's health naturally began to fail. He was a widower of long standing, his wife having died years before after decades spent in and out of the local state hospital. I'm told she was quite insane. It is my humble and unsubstantiated opinion that her "fire-breathing" husband helped make her that way. The couple had also lost their only son in WWII. That probably didn't help, either.

Being members of a close-knit community ensured that whenever Cousin Gillis's wife, Viola, was on furlough from the hospital, she'd have someone to help take care of her. In her last years, her minister husband was in high demand. He spent a lot of time in revivals and associations and such, counting on Mama to keep an eye on his wife. One Sunday while Mama was with her, Cousin Viola passed away. I never knew what from. I didn't think insanity was necessarily deadly.

Years went by. For many of them Cousin Gillis managed to function quite well by himself. He finally did begin to have medical problems, not too serious at first and still needing only minimal assistance with chores such as cooking and laundry. My mother took care of those things for him, often pressing us into service to help. We'd go over to Cousin Gillis's house two or three afternoons a week, spending an hour or two helping Mama tend to his needs. We'd sometimes help her make dinner, then we'd all share the meal.

Mama was a busy woman, so we kids helped out whenever and however we could. Not always by choice. Some of us were more helpful than others. Me, I was just a kid, so I wasn't good for much at all. Sister Girl wasn't too energetic, so she wasn't much help, either. Pete, by then, had already started practicing his cooking skills, so he was as handy as pockets on an apron, far outranking us his younger sisters with his culinary abilities.

One day Mama felt poorly, so she sent us over to Cousin Gillis's by ourselves, charging us with the task of cleaning his house and finishing his dinner. She had prepared a pot of fresh vegetables and cornbread, so all we had to do was fry the chicken for our cousin. Pete was the only one of us three kids who had any idea about how to fry a chicken, having done it once or twice before. My mother trusted him; so did we. Some things you just have to learn about.

When we got to Cousin Gillis's house Sister Girl and I set about straightening up. He was a neat old codger, so there wasn't a lot to do. We gathered up his dirty laundry, cleaned his bathroom, swept the floors, etc. Meanwhile, Pete was in the kitchen slaving over a hot stove. Cousin Gillis still used a wood burning Chamber's stove in those days, so Pete really was "slaving over a hot stove."

It wasn't long before Sister Girl and I detected the wonderful aroma of frying chicken, we could hardly wait. It wasn't until we sat down at the table for our meal that we noticed that something was not quite right.

The plump chicken was cut up nicely, sectioned just right and all. The coating was nice and thick, but something was amiss— the color of the fried chicken was just a tad off. Instead of a nice golden color, the chicken was a pasty kind of yellow. We weren't quite sure what to make of it, thinking maybe this was a new breed of fowl. (Foul was more like it.) We quickly dismissed this notion.

Pete and Marilyn

They didn't make chicken like this. Besides, we had seen the bird before Pete had cooked it—it had had looked fine, just like any other chicken.

We each served ourselves vegetables, bread and chicken, and filled our glasses to the rim with poly-pop. When the platter of chicken passed in front of Cousin Gillis, he speared a chicken breast with his fork, picking it up with a strange look on his face. We were sitting quietly, food untouched in spite of our intense hunger and ravenous greed, waiting for the adult's reaction.

Cousin Gillis laid the chicken breast on his plate, looked up at Pete and asked gently, "What did you fry the chicken in, Pete?"

Pete quickly replied, a sheepish look on his face, "I used your black iron skillet."

The rest of us sat expectantly, still as statues. We didn't know what Pete had done to the chicken, but we were certain it hadn't gotten this odd color from being fried in the iron skillet. Everybody used iron skillets to fry not only chicken but everything else as well. Yet, nowhere had we ever seen anything fry up like this.

"I didn't mean what kind of skillet did you use, Pete, I meant 'what did you put on the meat?'"

Pete didn't hesitate; he knew how to fry a chicken, by Jove! "I dipped it in beaten egg and flour." We sat a little straighter in our chairs, waiting for the queries and rebuttals to continue.

"Where did you get the flour?" Cousin Gillis was going somewhere with this, we just knew it. Instead of answering, Pete got up from his place and walked over to the cabinet nearest the stove. We watched closely as he picked up a tan paper bag of flour. Pete turned around and headed back to the table with the bag.

Cousin Gillis took one look at the bag and looked into poor Pete's innocent eyes. "Read the bag, Pete." Pete glanced down at the bag he was still holding in his hand, not really expecting to see anything unusual. Flour was flour, after all.

"What?!" He couldn't believe what he was reading. He had been so sure he knew what he was doing. He simply couldn't fathom how he had mistaken the bag of wheat wallpaper paste for flour. This was wallpaper paste! Sister Girl and I looked almost simultaneously down at our pieces of chicken. Yep! That would explain that pasty color—it came from paste.

Cousin Gillis took another look at Pete's stricken face. "It's okay," he said. "I have done worse myself. Besides, it was my fault for leaving this bag of paste in the kitchen." No matter what he said, though, Pete knew it was his own fault for not paying attention to what he was doing. He had been so sure of himself, so eager to please that the actual writing on the bag had gone unnoticed. In truth, the wallpaper paste bag did strongly resemble a flour bag. The texture and consistency of the powder inside was exactly the same as regular unbleached flour, and the color was similar as well. After all, this was a wheat product, just like the flour we cooked with.

We didn't eat the chicken but the dogs had a wonderful meal. They didn't mind at all that they were eating a product meant to paste paper to walls. I worried for a while that their guts might stick together. I should have been worried about our own guts. Those green beans, carrots, and cornbread were all we had to eat. It did okay for a while, but we got hungry pretty quickly with no chicken flesh to stick to our ribs.

After we'd cleaned up the kitchen and finished our other chores we hurried home. Naturally, Sister Girl and I were anxious to tell everyone about the chicken fiasco. Pete even laughed about it himself. I don't think he was really tickled, though. I suppose it did teach him a lesson because he never messed up like that again. Years later I got laughed at and teased unmercifully for putting raw dried beans in a vegetable soup which was only going to cook for thirty minutes. That was a mistake I never repeated, either.

CHAPTER 9: THE LOCAL LANDSCAPE

The local landscape has changed since the early days, as all things do. Areas that used to be farm and ranch land—the rich sandy loam yielding all kinds of wonderful things—are now grown up in timber. There are few cow-roaming pastures, and there is not one horse or mule in the entire community. The roads that used to be plain old red dirt are covered with asphalt.

The asphalt and the indoor plumbing are improvements. The rest . . . I'm not so sure. I am sure, though, that no one misses the way the roads were back then. When it was dry there was dust everywhere; you could easily tell when a vehicle was approaching by observing the unmistakable spirals of billowing rusty dust. When it rained these same cars and trucks slipped and sloshed on the red dirt roads, creating deep grooves called "ruts." Whenever you had to drive on a sloshy road you had to keep at least one of your wheels in the ruts. If you didn't, you were subject to slide into the ditch. If yours was the first vehicle on the road after a big rain you'd have a bit more difficulty, but not too much.

These ruts had been driven in for years and years, with each new rain ensuring the permanence of the grooves. When the rains stopped and the dust began to fly, the ruts were covered over, silent until the next sprinkles of rain. The next shower would bring the ruts out again, their deep imprints ready to guide you. It didn't matter if the trails were not immediately visible to you; if you slid around long enough you were bound to find one. All you had to do once your wheels were safely entrenched in a pattern was to give the car a little gas every now and then, but not too much or your car might sail up out of the rut and you'd find yourself in a ditch anyway. There wasn't a lot of room for mistakes.

The roads today are barely wide enough for two cars to pass. Whenever that occasion arises drivers must divide their concentration between waving at the passengers in the approaching vehicle and staying out of the deep ditches edging the road. Even more perilous than the ditches are the large trees lining the roads. It would be easy to concentrate too closely on vigorous waving and find yourself meeting up with a large yellow pine tree. To my knowledge, that never happened in our community. It did happen to a couple of our residents when they were visiting other areas. I suppose everyone knows best those roads and trees which grace their own neighborhoods. When they venture out, confusion sets in.

The general store was by far the most popular hang-out in our small, close-knit rural community. Well, really it was the only hang-out unless you counted the church which was situated just across the road.

It seemed sacrilegious to think of County Line Missionary Baptist Church as a hang-out, so we never considered our church in that light. It probably would have been all right for the Southern Baptists, but the more conservative Missionary Baptists hold themselves to less lenient standards.

It was not to the church that we turned for basic entertainment. Rather, the store was *the* place to be on Saturday. Community residents hung out at the store morning, noon and night. My paternal uncle, Claude Upshaw, owned and operated the general store. He had an ancient black and white RCA television, surely the prototype, and an even older brown, plastic tabletop Philco radio. That's it. There was no jukebox, no pool table, no dance floor, no record player. Likewise, there were no magazines, newspapers, or comic books. There was nothing to draw people to the store except amiable fellowship and innocuous amusement. The eclectic selection of stocked groceries and dry goods was an added bonus, an excuse to go to the store even if there was no real need. The opportunity for socialization was the real motivation for frequent trips to the store.

Claude did a brisk business for many years, maintaining his position as top grocer for the community by virtue of the relatively large size of his store and the wide variety of items available. The only competition was a tiny store owned and operated by Mister-Brother Ed Bagley.

Mister-Brother Ed was our cousin Leonia's husband. He catered to the younger clientele by stocking a wide variety of cookies and penny candy. He was not a serious contender for the mainstream grocery market. Mister-Brother Ed's name was, of course, not really "Mister-Brother Ed." His name was simply Ed Bagley. The added moniker came about because we children often heard Ed referred to as 'Brother Ed" by his like-minded deacon compatriots and other members of our church. Respectful youngsters that we were, we knew we should never address an elder without attaching a title. In our ignorance, tempered with vast respect, mind you, we adroitly combined the standard "mister" with the "brother" we heard our parents use.

For years and years—always, in fact—we called our Cousin Leonia's husband Mister-Brother Ed. Mama told us time and time again to select one title: either Mister or Brother, and use it alone. But, it was too late and the double title stuck. He was Mister-Brother Ed until the day he died. Then he became the Late Mister-Brother Ed, yet another handle added to his name.

We went to Mister-Brother Ed's store when we had just a few pennies. The cookies he carried tasted better than Uncle Claude's, and we got a lot more for our money. The huge plastic bins set atop Mister-Brother Ed's counter held a veritable feast of goodies beneath their red metal lids. There were rectangular coconut cookies, round chocolate cookies, stage planks with pink icing outlining their design, and several varieties that had no redeeming virtue except sugar. That was all that mattered.

Uncle Claude stocked cookies in his store, too, but not in abundance like Mister-Brother Ed did. Claude concentrated on basic foodstuffs. He carried no produce, cold-cuts or other perishables, just the basic staples: sugar, flour, meal, salt, baking powder, sardines, crackers (but no bread), and the like. In those days sardines and crackers were considered staples.

Uncle Claude knew what it took to run a successful operation, and he pretty much stuck with what worked—the basics. Every now and then he got a wild hair and stocked a few boxes of Betty Crocker cake mix or perhaps a case or two of Wolf brand tamales. We considered those foods exotic gourmet treats. Customers were always excited when Uncle Claude went out on a limb like that.

One time Uncle Claude went too far. He enterprisingly purchased a huge case of Kotex brand sanitary napkins. We girls were shocked to think that our elderly relative knew what Kotex was, much less had the nerve to buy some. I, for one, was so disconcerted and embarrassed by his boldness that I staunchly refused to buy or even acknowledge the existence of the big blue and white box. The carton of personals was stored behind the counter underneath the ledge that held the huge oak and glass candy display case. Stowed, they were out of sight of casual browsers. Supposedly, the discreet location lessened the embarrassment connected with making such purchases. In reality, placing the box behind the counter compounded the problem, since it meant that the purchaser had to go behind the counter to get the merchandise. Uncle Claude almost always sat behind the counter and saw everything that went on back there. We young women were so stupidly self-conscious that using white cotton rags seemed a more pleasant solution. Fortunately, there was only the one case of Kotex, and when that was gone, no more were ordered.

I never knew what happened to the contents of the large cardboard carton. Did they dry-rot, or did other females, bolder than me, actually buy up all the product? I certainly never asked.

Our community shopkeeper was an ordinary fellow. There was nothing fancy about him or his business, except for the interesting pricing strategy he employed. Behind that "regular guy" façade whizzed a capitalistic mind capable of competing with the best of them. Uncle Claude was adept at making money. With far-reaching vision, or perhaps by happen-stance, he created a monopoly in the local retail market by knowing how to keep his customers happy. "Give 'em what they think they need all of the time, and what they think they want some of the time" was his frequently espoused view. "They'll keep coming back." The reality was that we locals had little choice. The nearest supermarket was twenty miles away and it usually was not worth the effort to shop elsewhere. To his credit Uncle Claude did a respectable job of shop-keeping, managing to serve the community while ever cognizant of the almighty bottom line. One factor in his success was the careful management of inventory.

Every month or so Uncle Claude pulled out the spiral-bound notebook in which he recorded a running list of items needed to restock the store. The notebook was just like the ones we school kids used for our homework, except, for some inexplicable reason, his always had a red cover. I suppose that next to green, red was Uncle Claude's favorite color. The notebooks were filled up and discarded on a regular basis. When a new one was pressed into service it was all neat and clean, its pages straight and crisp. After being handled by a dozen or so people, having entries written in and later erased or scratched out, dropped on the floor time and again and so forth, it too began to take on a grungy appearance. The way it looked did not concern my uncle; the notebook was used until all its pages were filled. Only then was it thrown away. His use of notebooks was a testament to my uncle's frugality. We just called him stingy.

The notebook was an important tool in the operation of the store. Restocking occurred once a month or so; therefore, inventory of certain items was sometimes depleted several weeks before being replenished.

The notebook enabled us to keep tabs on what we had run out of as well as what was close to being sold out. There were other uses for the book, too. Customers often requested items they either wanted to see carried in the store on a routine basis, such as light brown sugar, or things simply needed for the short term, such as home-canning supplies. Uncle Claude sometimes conceded the need for the item and added it to his list. Often as not he simply picked up one or two of the requested items from one of the larger stores in town. Naturally, he would then jack up the price before selling it to the customer who had made the request.

I always wondered about this routine. It seems to me it would have been easier and certainly cheaper for the customer to just go to town and do what my uncle did—buy the item at the supermarket.

Once the shopping list was revised to suit him, no staples left off and the occasional exotic item carefully listed, Uncle Claude donned a fresh pair of pants and a clean plaid shirt. He never wore anything different.

His uniform was khaki pants or chinos for everyday wear, and he wore them every Sunday to church, adding a tie if the occasion warranted. Such cases included major church activities like homecoming Sunday, revivals and so forth, as well as the occasional wedding and more frequent funeral. Sometimes he traded a plaid shirt for a striped one, but he never wavered from the basic uniform.

After brushing the sparse white down atop his head which he fondly and whimsically called hair, Uncle Claude collected his walking sticks (or crutches—horses, he called them) and his wallet. The wallet was so choked with bills that it was held closed with rubber bands. Uncle Claude then climbed into his old blue and white International pickup truck and headed to the grocery warehouse.

The warehouse was located in the small college town of Nacogdoches, our county seat. It served as the main supply house for several grocery stores, such as Uncle Claude's. There was an extensive and varied inventory: canned goods, flour, sugar, meal, cake and other mixes, puddings and Jello, dog and cat food, and so forth.

Candy and cookies could be purchased from the warehouse, too, but my uncle usually ordered those items from the candy man. The "candy man" was a salesman who represented several candy manufacturers. He drove a large panel van right up to the store twice a month. Inside were dozens and dozens of different kinds of candies and cookies stacked against the walls of the van and covering the floor. Uncle Claude verbally gave his order and the salesman brought the cartons and boxes right into the store.

Soda was purchased similarly from a representative where it was bottled. Soda water came to us on big trucks loaded with cases of bottles and cans of Coke, Dr. Pepper, Fanta fruit flavors, Royal Crown Cola, and other flavors. It was quite a sight to see that big soda truck lumbering down the road, kicking up spirals of thick red dust as the big wheels chewed into the hard earth. We could hear it coming from a mile away.

The men who drove the trucks were always very friendly fellows, and husky too, able to sling case after case of soda onto their two-wheeled dollies as if they weighed nothing. They did all the work while my uncle sat on his stool and watched, chatting a running stream all the while. He wasn't expected to help unload the trucks. After all, he was the customer and was in no shape to handle the physical labor even if he had a mind to do so, which he did not.

For as long as I knew him, Uncle Claude walked with crutches or sticks or some combination of the two . . . his horses. Without that assistance he could amble a bit, but not for more than a few yards. Even with the crutches he walked with a slow and laborious gait, bending from the hip while rhythmically swinging his wooden assistants.

Occasionally, Uncle Claude surprised us. Exhibiting considerable spirit, he danced an interesting jig to music he made himself. Tuneless ditties rolled off his tongue, and mindless whistled tunes accompanied the tap-tap of his horses as they struck the floor. Most of the time his crutches were his dance partners, but every now and then he opted to partner the nearest door handle.

We laughed and laughed at the sight of our sixty-plus-year-old uncle twirling his plump, crippled body round and round. He balanced first on one crutch or stick and then the other, tapping them loudly against the planks of the hard wood floor. We found the scene hilarious but the truth is, he got an even bigger kick out of it. It seemed Uncle Claude did his best and most creative dancing as he was about to leave the store. Perhaps the excitement of leaving the community lightened his mood.

Leaning on his crutch, Uncle Claude shook and twisted his large behind like a bee buzzing around a favored blossom. I suppose he realized how ridiculous he looked, because he laughed even louder at his shenanigans than we did. Sometimes he danced all the way down the three short steps to the ground and then the twenty or so feet to the driver's side door of his truck, still laughing as he opened the door and climbed in. Now, *that* was something to see.

The store was padlocked and unavailable for business while its owner was out doing his shopping and attending to other business. The store was the only building in the area that was ever locked other than at night, or when the resident was going to be away for a while. We lived in a small, friendly community filled with harmless kinfolk, but my uncle was mindful of the possibilities. He lived in the three rooms just off the back side of the store. His private quarters consisted of a bedroom, kitchen, and bathroom.

His private rooms, along with the store, contained most of my uncle's worldly possessions. He had worked hard to acquire them and had no wish to be parted from any of it. It would not have been particularly wise to walk off and leave the door to such goodies unlocked even in our little enclave so before he left, Uncle Claude always made sure his front door was secured.

On the other hand, the single-paned, double-hung windows had nary a lock in sight. Some were nailed shut, many were not. This situation added little to the general security of the store. The fact that the padlock on the door was itself a very simple affair—swing hinges attached with screws driven directly into the door frame—might lead one to wonder how many times the store was burglarized. After all, the entire community knew exactly when Uncle Claude was and was not in residence. His locks and windows were a pitiful deterrent to even the most stupid and bumbling thief. Even so, the store was never burgled.

Robbery was almost out of the question. Only an idiot would try robbery in the daytime, and since Uncle Claude lived in the building (along with his shotgun collection), only a bigger idiot would try something in the nighttime, even under the cover of darkness. He was a very light sleeper. One would have to have been more than stupid to try and steal from Uncle Claude. At the time, there were few idiots in East Texas—a situation now much changed.

A gentler, kinder soul never lived, but there was little doubt in anyone's mind that Claude was capable of blowing a body to smithereens. Anyone foolish enough to try and part this normally affable man from his money would have quickly discovered that though he liked to frolic, he could be deadly serious.

When Uncle Claude arrived at the grocery supply house he gave the clerk his list, backed his truck up to the loading dock, and waited while the workers loaded his cargo bed with the goods he wanted. Sometimes he got out of his pickup and strolled—if you could call it that—around the giant warehouse, looking to see what new products were available. Occasionally, some new merchandise caught his eye and he bought it even though it was not on the sacred list.

Uncle Claude's rheumatism crippled him pretty badly in the hips and knees, so he rarely did much walking. He would drive his old truck all day long, traveling all over our own and neighboring counties. But if where he wanted to go required walking more than a few yards, he simply did not go. To spark a bit more business, sometimes the grocery manager would bring new items to the truck for my uncle to sample or take a look at. That was fine with Claude, as long as he was not the one doing the walking.

The loaders quickly finished piling the boxes, crates, bags, and cartons into the truck. Uncle Claude fished the required amount of currency from his fat wallet, paid his bill in full, and went on his way. The old International groaned and squeaked, burdened with the extra weight.

Because of the load, the trip home necessarily took a bit longer than the trip into town. Uncle Claude, never a speedy driver in any case, crept along at a leisurely pace, taking an hour or more to return home. Back at the store, handy nieces and/or nephews were rounded up to unload the heaping truck bed.

Once the groceries and other goods were stacked inside the store, Uncle Claude again pressed some hapless relative into service, pricing and putting away the goods. That tedious and physically challenging chore often fell to me. For hours I unpacked crates, bags, and cartons and artfully arranged the items on the homemade wooden shelves lining the walls of the store, or in the various display cases scattered around the interior. Putting away the supplies took an interminable three or four hours, less if one or more of my cousins or siblings was available to help me. The chore might have been less time-consuming except for his creative pricing strategy. Uncle Claude had his own way of doing things, and, try as I might, I was never able to convince him of an easier or more consistent method.

Goods came from the grocery supplier in bulk; they were not pre-priced and, of course, bar coding had not been invented yet. All the pricing and labeling was done at the retail establishment. If there were like items already on the shelf, I found the price and marked the new items with the same figures, occasionally raising the price to balance with inflation. As long as Uncle Claude left me alone, pricing the merchandise was a simple matter.

This done, I then positioned the fresh goods right in there with the old ones, never having heard the term "rotating stock." To my credit I did try to make the displays attractive through creative arrangement. Sometimes the items survived my attempt at artful merchandising; sometimes they simply toppled over.

Uncle Claude's creative pricing came into play when there were no samples on the shelves. If the item was completely sold out I would have to ask for a price. One would think that in such cases Uncle Claude would have consulted his bill of lading, invoice, inventory sheet, or something to cue him as to how much the item should retail for. No such thing! Uncle Claude looked at the item, thought a moment or two, and gave me his answer. He did not figure percentages of mark-up or use any other commonly employed mathematical equation to determine the retail price. He arbitrarily determined a number that seemed appropriate to him, and I never argued. It was his business after all, and I was just a hired hand. His methods evidently worked for him. He was not a poor man.

Everything Uncle Claude sold was priced in either even dollars or multiples of ten cents. For example, a soda water was a dime, a box of sardines thirty cents, a five-pound bag of sugar one dollar and fifty cents, and so on. Nowhere did I ever see a price ending in anything but zero; Uncle Claude did not operate that way. One reason was that he had no calculator or adding machine.

For years he used a homemade wooden drawer located underneath the counter as his cash register. The drawer was separated into three parts by two pieces of one-by-six-inch boards. One section of the drawer held bills in various denominations. One was for change, and the other contained bits of scrap paper, receipts, and so forth.

Uncle Claude eventually bought a used cash register, but it was so outdated that we could never figure out how to use it properly. For the entire history of the store's some forty years of operation, all the accounting was done manually. Uncle Claude never charged taxes on anything; consequently, adding and subtracting charges, and making change was simple. Aiding the simplicity was

Playing Dominoes at Uncle Claude's Store

the fact that all merchandise was priced in round numbers. After the re-stocking was completed, Uncle Claude treated his helpers to bottles of soda. Sometimes he added a candy bar or peanuts. Of course, he paid us, too, but after all that hard, sweaty, dusty work there was nothing we wanted more than a bottle of ice-cold Royal Crown Cola with a package of Planter's peanuts poured into it. It was such fun to watch the soda foam up in reaction to the salt from the nuts. We had to take the first drink quickly before the soda foamed over the top of the bottle. When the soda bottle was about half-empty the peanuts began to slide out of the bottle and into our mouths. With a little shake, more nuts were dislodged. Once the soda was completely gone any nuts left in the bottle would have to be coaxed out. Sometimes the efforts were unsuccessful and the bottle was returned to the soft drink company with nuts in the bottom.

The ideal situation was to finish the soda at the same time the last peanut slid into your mouth. It took real experience to accomplish this. Thinking back, I find it amazing that none of us choked. It never happened to anyone we knew, and for years peanuts in soda was a particularly welcome afternoon treat.

Young children drank fruit-flavored soda: grape, peach, or strawberry. After we got to be about twelve years old we could drink colas, but even then we were not allowed to drink "short" Cokes. You had to be much older to do that.

Back in those days the grown-ups did not allow kids to drink the Coke which came packaged in the diminutive 6.5 ounce bottles. I suppose they actually believed that the company was still putting cocaine in its product, but limiting this dispensation to the small bottles. As if even a huge conglomerate like Coca-Cola could afford to routinely spike its soft-drink with cocaine!

I understand Coke had done just that in the past, supposedly ending the practice when the dangers of spiking soft drinks with

hard drugs were uncovered. Assuming they ever did it, they probably stopped when the cost of cocaine became more and more
outrageous.

We young-uns weren't interested in short Cokes anyway. At
Uncle Claude's store, the bantam bottles of Coke cost just the same
as their heftier counterparts. No kid in his right mind spent his
dime to get less soda, no matter how much cocaine it might have
contained. We knew nothing and cared nothing about cocaine
anyhow, so there was absolutely no incentive for us to waste our
money buying short Cokes.

Our parents probably did not know what cocaine was, either.
No one ever actually said the short Cokes had cocaine in them.
What they said was that short Cokes were too strong for children.
I never found out where its strength lay. Back then, children did
not question the wisdom of the elders, so we never asked why the
soda was too strong. They said it was, and so it was.

Years later I determined that this "strong short Coke" theory
was pure fallacy. A more probable explanation is that the older
folks were attempting to justify spending the same amount to get
less product. Selling short Cokes was not big business at the store.
There were only one or two customers who insisted on drinking it.
I longed to ask those people why they preferred drinking 6.5 ounces
of Coke to drinking twelve ounces. I never did, though. As I mentioned, back then children did not question the presumed wisdom
of their elders. Second, there is the power of suggestion. Maybe
because they thought the stuff was spiked, they got a buzz from it.

Putting away his groceries was not the only chore I did for
him. Uncle Claude was, for all practical purposes, a single man.
His wife had left him years before and moved to Louisiana. They
never bothered with a divorce, and he and Aunt Idell remained
friends. She visited her estranged husband occasionally, but she
never stayed long enough to end Uncle Claude's bachelorhood.

My uncle could cook a bit, but he was certainly no culinary genius. Neither was I, though even as an adolescent I *fancied* myself a rather good cook (many years before I actually became one). To someone tired of his own cooking, variety is almost as good as skill. I might not have been able to cook very well, but I was willing to learn and I enjoyed experimenting with food. That, coupled with my availability, made me Uncle Claude's favorite cook.

On many occasions, I cooked at the store. I fried up canned mackerel or fresh chicken, fish, beef, whatever was handy. Sometimes, I messed up badly, but most of the time Uncle Claude ate my cooking in silence. Every now and then he complimented my efforts.

The liberal use of salt made the food I prepared more palatable to him. Uncle Claude loved his salt and put it on just about everything he ate. He salted his pork chops and his watermelon. He salted his bread and all the vegetables he ate. He used a lot of salt. No matter how much I put into the food while preparing it he inevitably added more. That he was hypertensive and diabetic did not deter him one bit. Uncle Claude loved his salt, and for years he used extreme amounts.

One time, I decided to help him end his habit of salting food before tasting it. It was my intention to so heavily salt the next dish I prepared for him that he would have no need to add any more. I wasn't being mean. I sincerely wanted to prepare tasty meals for him, and I believed that if I could only season food properly, he would be impressed with my cooking talent.

After school one day, I walked the half-mile from home to the store to cook my uncle's dinner. I laid out my wares and cut up the young, average-sized fryer while oil heated in the heavy iron skillet. I seasoned the chicken thoroughly. I added seasoning befitting a large turkey or small side of beef. There was probably a third of a cup of salt in the frying batter. Again, I was not trying to punish my uncle in any way. I only wanted his confidence that I had finally learned how to properly season his food.

The chicken fried up nicely, as golden and crisp as any I had ever seen, tender and juicy on the inside, with a lovely crust covering it. It looked like a Crisco commercial. When it was all done I artfully arranged several pieces on a colorful platter, serving it up with fresh green beans. They were thoroughly seasoned as well. I added beautiful wedges of freshly baked and buttered corn bread. I proudly carried the platter from the kitchen to my uncle's perch behind the counter. He grinned when he saw me coming.

I set the platter on the counter in front of my uncle, fully intending to warn him not to reach for the salt shaker he kept just inside the display counter. I had not considered the element of speed. Uncle Claude hurriedly picked up his favorite shaker, the one with the extra-large holes, and proceeded to shake. He shook and shook. He was so fast with the salt shaker that before I could tell him I didn't think this chicken was going to need any additional seasoning, he had already coated the bird.

I watched in horror as more and more grains of salt sifted through the large holes of the shaker. I had not been prepared for this. I never thought he could take that salt shaker in hand and sprinkle so fast. He never did anything fast. Yet here he was sprinkling furiously, ruining the chicken before I could utter a word of warning.

I was appalled, and could do nothing but swallow and swallow again, searching vainly for words as the ability to speak completely deserted me. Moments and an eternity later I realized there was little point in saying anything. The reality of the situation would soon make itself apparent. Uncle Claude picked up a juicy chicken leg, opening his big mouth wide as he bit off a sizable plug. As he started to chew, his entire countenance changed. Uncle Claude's face, which had reflected delight at the prospect of a tasty meal, metamorphosed into first puzzlement and then astonishment, even while chicken grease glossed his full lips.

I stood immobile. He chewed a bit longer, slowing with each successive motion. He knew what had happened. He stopped chewing. Uncle Claude genteelly picked up his fork, slid it into his mouth. Out came the wad of partially masticated chicken. He laid the bolus on his platter and looked up at me.

"You got the chicken too salty," he said.

The audacity of the man astounded me. "No!" I exclaimed, determined to set the record straight. "*You* got the chicken too salty." Not to be outdone, Uncle Claude picked up a fresh piece of chicken, plucked all the skin off, taking the added salt with it, and handed the stripped meat to me.

"Try it," he said. I began to get the feeling that perhaps I had been a little heavy with the salt. Cautiously, I reached my hand out to take the proffered leg. I could feel my heart pounding as I took a small bite.

"Yuck!" I groaned, hurrying to the door. The salt permeated the chicken. Even with the fried skin removed, it was so salty it burned my mouth. All I could think about was getting rid of it.

I felt sick. I thought I was being so clever and, as a result, I had ruined my uncle's dinner. I had also ruined any chance of going home anytime soon. I knew what I had to do. Unbidden and unasked, I nevertheless felt duty bound to stay at the store long enough to prepare another entree for Uncle Claude.

There was no more chicken, so I made a cheese and onion omelet. I wasn't sure if Uncle Claude liked omelets but I knew he loved onions. The cornbread had escaped my salt bombardment and would go well with the eggs. I added no salt.

I reassembled the platter, substituting the omelet for the chicken and sliced onions with tomatoes for the overly-seasoned green beans. Uncle Claude was waiting. He didn't seem angry that I had ruined his dinner. I guess it took an awful lot to make him mad. As I sat the newly reconstructed meal on the counter, I explained that I had really tried to season the food properly. I apologized and promised to never get carried away with salt again.

With the platter of eggs and bread steaming, Uncle Claude reached automatically for his salt shaker. I was on my way back to the kitchen and could just see him out of the corner of my eye. I stopped in my tracks, turned around and stared. Uncle Claude noticed me standing there looking at him. He set the shaker down, picked up his fork and tasted the eggs. Only then did he salt his omelet—slowly. From where he sat, he could not see the smirk of my face as I continued toward the kitchen. I wasn't the only one to learn a valuable lesson that day.

Uncle Claude never mentioned the incident, at least not to me. I don't know if he told anyone else about it or not. I doubt it, though, because if any of my relatives had known, they would have teased me unmercifully about it.

He was a kind old guy who tended to be rather soft-hearted and always went out of his way to make people feel comfortable. Who else would let folks sit up in their place of business hour after hour and never comment on their minimal or non-existent purchases? He enjoyed the company.

On cold winter days and evenings the kin folks wandered in and out of the store, sometimes stopping in to pick up sugar or flour or other needed items. As often, people dropped by just to catch up on the latest gossip. Whatever the news was, good or bad, it was sure to pass through the store. We spent many hours gathered around the wood-burning stove visiting and watching television.

Some perched on the ladder-backed, cowhide-bottomed chairs scattered about. Others sat on upended wooden soda water crates.

Many tales were told and numerous rumors investigated while we congregated at the store. We enjoyed the fellowship, simple though it was. We never sang, we never played games; we never did any of those things. Yet, the store was the place to be.

The experiences we shared at the store went beyond having fellowship with one another. Way beyond. With the help of older relatives we were building and shaping our personalities, solidifying our values, determining our destinies.

Uncle Claude did not allow cursing or rude talk of any kind on the premises. There was no drinking, no fighting, no shouting. He never said not to do those things, but everybody who set foot in the store readily and without question accepted this code of conduct. This unspoken code existed not only for the store but for the rest of the community, as well. It was the standard of behavior in those days. Uncle Claude was a deacon, and the church was literally just across the road from the store. Perhaps this was a contributing factor to the way he ran his business.

When the weather was nice folks often sat outside on the hand-crafted wooden benches scattered here and there on the store's front porch. We younger folks spent the time playing in the yard in front of the store. We played hide-and-go-seek if it was dark enough. In the daytime we drew hopscotch courts in the dirt with a stick and played for hours on end. "Ring Around the Rosie" was another favorite. Occasionally we played school and "Simon Says." Our games were usually harmless, but every now and then our entertainment carried with it the potential for injury.

One time my cousins-nee-running buddies (Chee-Chee, Jeffie Mae and Big Sister) and my sister Marilyn (whose nickname was and is Sister Girl) decided to stage a contest. The game was to see who could swing from the exposed porch rafters for the longest amount of time. Whoever swung the longest without falling off would be declared the winner. Aunt Jeffie's grand-daughters

Chee-Chee, Jeffie Mae, and Big Sister were much leaner and lighter than Sister Girl and I, so it was a preconceived notion that one of them would win.

Each of us in turn jumped the short vertical distance to grab hold of the overhanging rafter, careful of the exposed splinters. After everyone else had swung for as long as they could, it was my turn.

I grabbed the rafter with both hands and began swinging. Jeffie Mae pushed me once or twice to boost my momentum. I held on with all my might and had begun to believe I might be able to win the contest. Pride does go before a fall, and that's just what happened. I got proud—and then I fell.

My hands started slipping just as I was about to reach a very respectable forty-five seconds of hang time. I smugly congratulated myself on my physical strength and equally strong character. I might have managed to hang on, but just as I began to slip Jeffie Mae, thinking I had slowed down because I had run out of steam, decided I needed another push. There was no way for her to know that I had slowed down in order to regain my grip. I was in trouble. It was the third shove that did it. She pushed and down I went. I hit the ground landing on my backside so hard that I literally bounced. It hurt, and I knew I would never swing from those rafters again.

My partners crackled with unconcealed glee until they considered that I might have been injured. To their credit, the other girls managed to stifle their giggles long enough to determine that I wasn't in danger of dying immediately. With barely contained snickers they dragged me to my feet and dusted me off. I was not amused.

"What's going on out there?" The adults inside the store had heard the commotion. We knew that if we confessed to injury our fun evening would be over, cut short because of our parents' concern for our safety.

I had no choice. I shouted with teeth clenched against the pain. "Nothing. . . . We just knocked over some soda water crates." A bald-faced lie to be sure, but telling the truth would not have benefited anyone. I was less than mortally wounded, uninjured really, and we all wanted to keep playing.

The fun continued, but none of us ever swung from the rafters again. We were young. We were foolish. We were not stupid.

CHAPTER 10: INJURIES

We children were blessed not to sustain mortal or even serious injuries. Rarely were there more than a few scrapes and bruises, even when we were at our most boisterous. Accidents did happen, though, such as the time Big Sister broke her collarbone. No one in our clique had ever broken anything before, so we were all highly intrigued by the injury. We pestered Deborah constantly.

"How does it feel?" we asked. "Let me see your sling again." "How do they do an X-ray?" On and on we went, question after question repeated in our quest for more knowledge.

Deborah had been playing on the back of her grandmother's (my Aunt Jeffie) truck. Somehow she missed the jump cue shouted out to her by one of her siblings. Not hearing the verbal instruction affected her timing, causing her to jump too quickly—before she was fully prepared. Instead of landing on the soft dirt she hit a tree stump, banging her left shoulder hard against the remains of what had once been a pin oak tree. Boy, did she howl! Aunt Jeffie took her to the hospital where she received a shoulder sling and pain medication. She wore the sling for several weeks but eventually recovered without incident. She stopped jumping off trucks.

There was also the time her sister Chee-Chee was spurred in the face by a rooster. I don't know what kind of game she was trying to play with him, but he obviously did not understand the rules. The rooster's talon scratched her so badly that thirty years later she still bears the scar.

It seems, now that I think about it, that Chee-Chee received more injuries than the rest of us. She came to school one day with a ghastly looking black eye. We were astonished, certain that Aunt Jeffie had finally cracked under the strain of raising her grandchildren. We were relieved to learn that no one had hit her. Chee-Chee assured us that she had fallen off an old hump-back trunk while using it as an elevated stage for her musical revue. The song she was singing got cut rather short after she hit the floor. Her hairbrush microphone sailed even further through the air than she did, finally coming to rest some twenty feet away.

Sister Girl was not without her share of injuries, either. Her nemesis was nails—not the kind you polish and file, but the steel ones used in construction. If there was an old rusty nail sticking up anywhere in all of County Line, she would find a way to step on it. She stepped on a nail just about every summer. We would be playing, running around barefoot, prancing and jumping when, sure enough, her bare foot would sense a nail close by and step on it. The pain must have been extreme. She cried and cried, moaned and groaned. But what she did not do was stop stepping on nails.

We were sympathetic, amazed that any one person could find so many rusty nails to accidentally step on. For sure these were accidents. No one, and I mean no one crazy or sane deliberately steps on rusty nails. She never saw a doctor for her puncture wounds. We took our chances with Ptomaine poisoning and other potential sequelae to such injuries. Sister Girl was luckier than some we knew of. She never contracted lockjaw, gangrene, or anything. Her good fortune must have been due to the turpentine Mama liberally applied to her injury, one of her many home remedies.

After Sister Girl's foot found its mark she managed to hobble into the house, seeking out Mama and the turpentine bottle. If we were out of the smelly stuff Mama promptly dispatched one of us to the store to fetch a fresh bottle. Mounds of scientific evidence now substantiate the benefits of turpentine. I suspect that Sister Girl's quick and uneventful healing had more to do with Mama's liberal use of prayers than with the medicinal value of turpentine.

Mere days after her injury Sister Girl was up and about, having shed the white rag her foot had been bandaged with, ready to run and play again. She usually stepped on only one nail per season. I am not sure how that came about, but I'd say that she was motivated to pay closer attention to where she set her feet. After all, no one wanted to miss out on the summer fun. If one were sick or hurt one simply had to stay at home and could not hang out with the rest of the kids. The injured party would be missed and her absence regularly was commented on, but not one of us was willing to keep company with a fallen comrade. We had things to do, playing mostly, but often going to church and hanging out at the store as well. There was no time or interest in playing nursemaid. That was the understood sentiment of the community's youth.

My other siblings and I did not escape injury, either. Even Sister Girl had more to contend with than the occasional puncture. I experienced a few, and Gus did as well.

When I was about eight years old, Missonnell bought or found, I don't remember which—although I would guess that considering the state of our finances, it was most likely found—an old, red, wooden rocking horse. He was an interesting specimen with his stringy black yarn hair and brown painted-on nose.

Butch brought the horse home to Gus who, spoiled brat that he was, allowed no one else to ride him. Gus loved that horse. Shouts of "Giddy-up" and "Whoa, whoa now" reverberated through the house day after day. The pleasure he got from riding that piece of wood was disgusting!

The horse got tired of Gus. I don't know if it was his selfishness in not allowing his siblings to ride that the horse found irritating or Gus's habit of making the poor animal buck time after time. In any case that lifeless, wooden beast found a way to get the boy off his back. He threw him.

I won't venture to guess how it may have happened, but somehow Gus fell or was thrown off the horse and in the process injured his personal anatomy. To the doctor they went, Mama, Missonnell and Gus. Injured nuts was one condition that warranted a trip to the physician, you see. The rest of us waited at home, anxious for their return. Gus had really done it this time. There was blood all over the floor, all over that horse, everywhere! At first we kids did not know exactly what part of his body Gus had injured. Judging from the copious amount of blood left behind, we surmised that the appendage in question was never going to work properly again.

They were gone for hours. It was a forty-five minute drive to the doctor's office so we expected it to take a while, but the minutes fairly crawled by. Pete, Tenchie, Sister Girl, and I were genuinely worried about our brother. The longer they stayed gone the more we worried, imagining the worst and finally deciding that the wounded part was so seriously injured that it required amputation.

After an eternity we heard the sound of our old car approaching. With trepidation we ran outside, anxious with concern and blatant curiosity. We watched with interest as Missonnell gingerly lifted Gus from the back seat and carefully carried him into the house. Questions poured from us. "What did the doctor say?" "Is he all right?"

Mama walked on into the house explaining as she went. "Well, he bruised his testes pretty badly."

"His what?" We thought testes were something you failed at school. We were on summer vacation, so this statement made no sense.

"Yes," Mama explained to us dunces, "he bruised his balls really badly." Oh . . . balls, *that's* what this is about.

Gus could not walk straight for weeks. We felt so bad for him that for a long time we let him get by with no teasing on the subject whatsoever. It was years before even Bubba, our older brother and by far the most clownish of us, teased Gus about his experience.

Missonnell got rid of the horse as soon as they got back from the doctor. I think the horse endured a flaming end as kindling for the wood stove. His revenge may have been sweet, but it was surely short-lived and very costly. Imagine a wooden horse having the audacity to throw someone. Hurrumph!

I believe Gus learned a lesson from that horse. Perhaps if he had been less selfish someone else would have been riding him when the horse decided he no longer wished to be a beast of burden.

For sure, a few years later Pete learned a lesson about greed and excess. Sometimes a little of a good thing is good enough, while a lot of a good thing might not be such a good thing after all.

While in junior high school Pete contracted the currently prevalent influenza. Mama and Missonnell did not take him to the doctor, as death was not imminent. He was sick, but he was not dying. It wasn't that our parents did not believe in professional medical intervention; they did, but they just did not avail themselves of it until it was necessary—absolutely necessary. For instance, respiratory arrest automatically qualified its sufferer a trip to the physician (or the next logical place.) Victims of respiratory arrest were qualified for several other things. He got a plush, completely outfitted, color coordinated permanent home and his own small piece of property. He also got a big party in his honor. He absolutely could not participate except as a very passive decorative item, a conversation piece, or as something to cry over.

Other non-life threatening respiratory ailments were treated with massive doses of Three Sixes liquid and mullein tea made with pine needles and leaves from the widely available mullein plant.

Pete had been in bed all day and, as a testament to how sick she believed him to be, Mama insisted he sleep in the "company" room. There was a pink chenille bedspread with scalloped edges and red rose inserts adorning the tall four-poster double bed. The furnishings in the room were the nicest in the house. It was always clean and neat with not even a fringe on the bedspread out

Pete

of place. We were jealous that Pete was allowed to spend the night in the room while we were not allowed in there. That room was Mama's pride and joy. No one but the most honored guests slept in the room. At other times the room was used when the older girls' boyfriends visited. They could "take company" in the room, but that was it.

When their boyfriends came, Sister Girl and I usually remained in the room as chaperones. I did not particularly care for spying on my older sisters, but Sister Girl reveled in it and took extreme pleasure in reporting to Mama everything that went on. I could be bribed and convinced to leave the room with just a stick of chewing gum. Sister Girl exacted a considerably heavier price. It did not take long for Early Ervin, Faye's beau, to figure this out. He always brought Juicy Fruit for both of us. It worked for me, but Sister Girl was much more tenacious. I don't know if it was because she took her duty more seriously than I, or if she simply wanted a bigger bribe than a stick of gum. I suspect it was the latter.

Anyway, with Pete ill, Mama decided that he would rest better in the guest room away from the crowd of our family. She helped him climb into the tall four-poster, gave him half an Anacin tablet, and tucked him in for the night. Mama only tucked us in if we were sick.

This event occurred long before children's Tylenol was developed. No one had even heard of Reye's Syndrome, the disease that sometimes strikes young people who are given aspirin products for fever. I wonder if Reye's Syndrome was engineered by the same folks who developed Tylenol. In any case, if we were sick, we took Bayer aspirin. If we were really sick we were given Anacin or Excedrin.

The Anacin seemed to do the trick, easing Pete's discomfort and allowing him to sleep, resting peacefully in never-never land. The rest of us—Mama, Butch, Gus, Sister Girl, Tenchie and I—remained in the living room watching the one channel we could get on our black and white RCA television. It would be hours before we discovered that Pete really did take a trip to never-never land.

It was a Saturday evening and time for the Mitch Miller show, *Sing Along with Mitch*. The only thing interesting about that music program was that we thought white Mitch Miller was married to colored Leslie Uggams (we were still "colored" back then). This was the Sixties, so such a thing was practically unheard of. Later, we learned that she was just his protégé. Uh-huh. Anyway, the show was not to our liking, no matter who was or was not wed to whom. We kids always took this opportunity to go outside and play "hide-and-go-seek," weather permitting. We played until the show went off and then came back into the house to watch whatever came on next, *Bonanza*, I think. When *Bonanza* went off we went to bed while our parents watched the ten o'clock news.

At about 2:00 AM we heard the unmistakable sound of an approaching truck. The truck slowed and stopped outside our house. We all got out of bed to see who could be stopping by at this time of night. Visitors or vehicular traffic after 10:00 PM usually meant there was a problem somewhere in the community. We were wrong.

Imagine our surprise when we opened the front door and saw Uncle Floyd's old black GMC truck parked outside. Uncle Floyd climbed out of his truck, and it was then we noticed that someone was with him. Mr. Freeley Roland, Aunt Odessa's father, got out of the truck, too. We also noticed another head poking up from the seat, one that strangely resembled Pete's. We knew it could not be Pete, though. After all, Pete was in bed asleep.

The two men helped the third person from the truck. Yep! It was Pete all right.

What in the world was Pete doing in the truck with Uncle Floyd and Freely Roland? How could he be here walking up the steps between the two men when he was in bed sick with the flu? The question went unspoken. Had Mama had twins and neglected to tell us, possibly giving the spare to Mr. Freeley and Miss Roxie, his wife, to raise? Had they then decided to bring their twin back to us for some reason?

Well, Uncle Floyd had quite a story to tell us, and it had nothing to do with twins. It seemed that his household was awakened when they heard someone screaming and yelling near their home. Uncle Floyd explained that he got up when he heard the racket and turned on the front porch light. The hundred-watt bulb was too weak to illuminate much of anything, so he hurriedly fetched his heavy-duty flash light and headed toward the cow pasture. Meanwhile Mr. Freeley, who was spending the night with his daughter and son-in-law, also got up to investigate.

Uncle Floyd said that at this point he knew that someone was in serious distress. As he got closer to the source of the noise he could see why. The trapped person was hopelessly entangled in his barbed wire fence and the bramble growing within it.

It was Pete thrashing wildly, grappling with the menacing wire, desperately trying to get loose. He screamed and yelled, and when Uncle Floyd asked what was the matter, Pete hysterically insisted that the moon was after him. He continued to struggle, his futile efforts entangling him more completely in the wire.

Uncle Floyd got close enough to assure Pete that the moon was not going to get him. Pete must have recognized his uncle because he calmed down enough for Uncle Floyd to free him. Mr. Freeley worked to free Pete's arms from the vines while Uncle Floyd dislodged his feet and legs from the barbed wire.

Pete had gotten himself so entangled that Uncle Floyd was forced to cut several strands of the barbed wire with wire cutters. With his father-in-law's help, Uncle Floyd was finally able to free Pete from the wire and bramble. He was bleeding slightly from the scratches on his hands and legs, but was mostly just scared and disoriented. The men took the boy into the house where Aunt Odessa gingerly removed the berry vines still stuck to his pajamas. She teasingly said later that she moved slowly and carefully because she didn't want Pete to mistake her for the cheese the moon is purported to be made of. "He may have been hungry," she added. Aunt 'Dessa cleaned Pete's scratches with alcohol, gave him a drink of water, and helped the men load him into the cab of the truck.

By the time Pete made it home he was sleepy, lethargic but no longer hallucinating. He was obviously tired (running from the moon is hard work) but, other than the scratches, he was fine. There was no doubt that Pete had been wildly hallucinating. The moon was full that night, very luminous in the clear sky, but I doubt that it had developed the power to pursue hapless adolescents. We queried Pete about why he had gotten out of bed and how he got to Uncle Floyd's house a half mile away. He could not tell us and was so exhausted that Mama soon ended the debriefing and sent him back to bed. This time Pete had to sleep with Tenchie. No more isolated company room for him. He never slept in there again, either.

The company room was in the front of the house parallel to the living room, and like the living room, it too had a door leading outside. It would be a very simple matter for someone to leave the room and go outside without anyone knowing it. This is apparently what Pete did. He was not sneaking out or anything of the kind. Rather, he was so involved with his nightmare that he was unable to control his actions and walked out of the house. Once outside, he imagined that the moon was pursuing him. That's when he ran away and became entangled in the fence surrounding our uncle's pasture.

The incident frightened Mama badly, and from that point on she never gave us Anacin or Excedrin again—not for any reason. If we had an ailment that could not be eased by plain old Bayer aspirin, we just had to tough it out. We all believed that Pete had demonstrated a severe reaction to one-half of an Anacin tablet, so we understood why Mama did not give us strong analgesics. We were his siblings, so there was good reason to fear that we would react to the medicine as Pete had.

It was not until many years later that the true causative factor was exposed. Pete was about thirteen when he had his psychotic experience, and he was nearly thirty before he told me the whole story about his wild night. He never did tell our mother. To this day, she thinks he is extremely sensitive to that class of analgesics. She teases him that he must always be very careful since we know for a fact that for him, psychosis lays just under the surface of sanity. Maybe she was not teasing. In any case Pete's confession explained his true culpability in the incident.

Pete told me that after Mama gave him the Anacin, he lay down and began to feel much better after a while. An hour or so later he decided that if half an Anacin tablet could make him feel so much better, then several more would make him completely well. He got up, found the bottle and took a dozen tablets. He went back to sleep. The nightmare woke him, but according to Pete he was so confused all he could do was try to escape. He could not say why he left the house but he remembered that once he got outdoors the moon "got after him." The next thing he knew, Uncle Floyd and Mr. Freeley were bringing him home.

I never knew how Uncle Floyd reacted to finding his nephew in that predicament. I imagine he reckoned that the family's pesky "crazy gene" had reared its ugly head again. It did that from time to time.

Uncle Floyd was a bit different from his siblings. He, too, was a kind and very generous man. He had a streak of independence that should have been an admirable trait, but these were the days of racial tension and blatant inequities. We were fortunate to have our own—the ability to thrive in an often hostile and always unequal environment. The circumstances, then as now, were not the best for those of color, but we strove to get along with those different from us. Though he was a peaceable man, Uncle Floyd took no quarter and gave none. It did not matter what color you were, he took no sh--! Uncle Floyd had a deep husky voice, which got deeper and huskier the madder he got. He'd cuss and stomp, flapping his tongue furiously between his three teeth as he ranted and raved. The recipient of his ire was usually one of his animals, a stubborn mule most likely, although he did unleash his fury on a stubborn person every now and then. Everyone within a hundred-mile radius knew not to mess with him. When Uncle Floyd got perturbed about something, you could hear him cussing a mile away. "Dad-blamed bastard . . . oughta cut his damned. . . ." That doesn't sound like much, not compared to the way people talk these days, but he was the only one of the brothers who cursed on a regular basis, once or twice a year.

Uncle Floyd was different in another way as well. He was skinny and had smallish feet. Not *small* feet, just smallish in comparison to his brothers. This meant that he did not have to special order his shoes from the Mason shoe company. He could buy them at a regular department store, something his siblings could not do. He was also the only one who never went to church. Not that one necessarily had anything to do with the other, but the fact was, he did not practice hypocrisy in any area.

I shudder to think what might have happened to Pete if the moon had chosen to chase him in another direction, away from Uncle Floyd's kind interception. East Texas is covered with forests, lakes and rivers, and there are many wild creatures about. The story could have ended very badly even though the moral would have been the same: sometimes more is definitely not better.

Gus and I were the youngest kids. As toddlers we shared everything from our favorite snack—cornbread mixed with buttermilk and sugar—to our childhood illnesses. Just about every little germ or virus ever engineered has at one time or another found its way into my system. I was a sickly youngster. *Puny*, my folks called me. Gus was not as delicate as I was, but he suffered right along with me on several occasions. I appreciated the company.

We were preschoolers when we got the mumps. My left jaw and neck were swollen, Gus's right. We looked like two of Alvin's (right and left) Chipmunks. It was a miserable time for both of us.

While we were sick our parents' folks fed us sardines and crackers. First, though, they rubbed the oil from the fish on our swollen jaws and necks, a common treatment back then. The jury is out concerning the efficacy of this treatment. Perhaps the theory was that if you stank bad enough the mumps would gladly flee. To this day the smell of sardines makes my throat swell and ache.

As soon as we recovered from the mumps we contracted the measles. Again, we lay in bed together as we endured not only the disease but the treatment. Later came chicken pox, along with the requisite gallons of calamine lotion and the warnings: "Don't you scratch those bumps. If you do you'll get the pox in your eyes and it will 'put your eye out.'" Now that's incentive!

Some ailments, illnesses, and accidents Gus and I had to suffer singularly. He never caught pneumonia from me, and I never got his whooping cough or croup. I suffered alone when I tore the cartilage in my right knee. I did not break his knee just so I would have my favorite suffering partner. Conversely, Gus did not lock me in the house with him when the curtains caught fire just so he would have someone to share smoke inhalation with. I am appreciative.

Gus and I were playing in Mama's company room one day. There we were, happy as little black clams, if there were such things, bouncing around on Mama's pride and joy, the big fluffy bed with the red and white chenille coverlet. Mama was outside doing chores and had no idea we were playing in the guest room. She never found out, either.

After we played for half an hour or so, I figured we had pressed our luck hard enough and decided to continue my entertainment in the out of doors. I was only four at the time but had already developed an uncanny intuition for when a whipping was close at hand. I knew if we got caught jumping on Mama's bed, this would be one of those times.

I jumped on the bed one last time, then suggested to Gus that it would be best for us to play outside. For some odd reason he decided not to follow me, surely a first for this notorious tag along.

I went into the front yard and began gathering China berries from the ground. We had a huge, sprawling tree in our front yard. I could hear Gus playing around inside the living room and called out for him to join me. "Come outside, Gus," I said. He never did. I continued tossing the hard green China berries. I threw them at the dogs, then the cats. The pets soon grew weary of my target practice and hid underneath the porch. I played solitarily for another ten minutes, content and happy to be outside.

Mama intuitively knew something was wrong. There was no smoke coming from the windows of the house, there were no unusual sounds, either. Yet, somehow, she knew all was not well. She was right. The house was on fire.

I stood in the yard under the China berry tree while Mama frantically dashed up the steps and onto the porch. She moved faster than I ever thought possible, but when she reached the front door she could not open it. The door was locked from the inside! Mama tugged and pushed, twisting and turning the doorknob. The door would not budge! Gus had shut the heavy steel deadbolt lock. We were locked out, and he was trapped inside!

"Gus, Gus. Unlock the door!" Mama screamed.

I joined in, adding my weak voice to Mama's shouts. Together we pleaded with Gus to unlock the door. By now we could hear Gus inside, crying. We could also hear the crackle of fire as the flames licked the wallpaper and climbed the curtains.

I ran to the nearest window. The curtains had fallen off their rods, consumed by the rapidly advancing fire. They lay in a heap on the floor, flames still dancing through them. As I peered through the smoky room, I saw Gus sitting on the old wooden box where we kept our toys. He was perilously close to the flames, too terrified to move. He was crying, and I was screaming. "Open the door! Open the door!" I was too young to know the full extent of the dangers, but I knew you could not sit so close to fire without it causing harm. Gus was sitting almost in the middle of flames. There was fire by his feet, fire by his head, fire all around him. And he was not moving.

I continued to plead with my baby brother to get out of the house. Meanwhile, Mama was engaged in more practical efforts. She filled five gallon buckets with water. These she sat on the ground beside the window. With the end of a garden rake, Mama broke the windowpane and immediately doused the flames nearest Gus. She opened the window and sat a second bucket of water inside.

A few moments later she herself climbed into the burning room. She used the second bucket of water to douse more flames. Hurriedly, she gathered Gus into her arms and hustled him out of the room.

Her baby safe, Mama could then address the fire at her leisure. Actually, if I remember correctly, my brother Eugene happened to come home. Or maybe he heard our screams from Uncle Hadie's home where he'd been visiting. Anyway, the fire was extinguished and Gus, miraculously, was uninjured.

The fire began in the chimney of the wood-burning stove. The damage was minimal, with nothing lost except the curtains and a section of wallpaper. It was not the first, nor would it be the last time we had a chimney fire. It was, however, the only time someone's life was at risk.

When Gus recovered from his fright, I asked him why he locked the front door in the first place. He said that he locked the door to keep me out. As if I had any interest in entering a burning house.

Gus said that when he realized the house was afire he tried to get out but could not release the tricky dead bolt. Frustrated and frightened, he sat down on the window seat and gave way to the most intense crying jag of his life.

Gus had lived in that house all his life but apparently never noticed that the house had three doors to the outside. I teasingly reminded him that if he had come outside with me he would not have been in the house when it caught fire. He would not have had to tolerate having Mama and me tell the story over and over about how he sat and cried as the house was burning around him.

This was not Rome, and Gus did not know how to play a fiddle.

CHAPTER 11: BORN AND RAISED: BIG HEADS, BIG FEET

I was born and raised as the almost last child amongst a host of others. There was nothing remarkable about my birth. I didn't weigh almost thirteen pounds like my baby brother Gus; I didn't cause unnecessary pain because of an unnaturally large head like my sister Byrd. I was just born!

We all had pretty big heads, but there was something special about Byrd's. My mother has said that she "liked to have never had her because of that noggin." Byrd's neighbor once teasingly told her that not only were we hard to deliver because of our big heads, but then our mother had to deliver our big feet as well.

We do, almost without exception, have rather large ones. Feet that is. In fact, finding shoes has long been a challenge for most of us girls. My sisters Maye and Marilyn (Sister Girl) thought they had died and gone to heaven when they discovered a shoe store in a Los Angeles suburb which catered to "big hoofed" folks. The store's trade name is "MFSB." When I visited the store I chanced a remark inquiring about the odd name. Sister Girl said that the initials stood for "mother, father, sister, brother," indicating the familial nature of the business.

Hurrumph! "More like, 'My Feet So Big.'" I couldn't resist the comment. I think Sister Girl was a bit offended. She went on to say they didn't just sell big shoes, they sold real little ones, too. It didn't matter what she said. I was sure the initials meant just what I said. The company should never have used those initials for their trade name, inviting such speculations as I had made.

Maye and Sister Girl were avid patrons, but I was never actually shod by that establishment. I had other sources. Running around in the red dirt of East Texas barefoot surely contributed to our foot size, but I must also credit our genetic makeup.

Our father is no small man, standing 6'3" tall and with a high weight of more than 300 pounds. Mama, on the other hand, was more normal—in height anyway—standing just over 5'4". That was perfectly okay, but for a long time after her first few children she herself weighed darn near 250 pounds. She started losing weight when I was about five years old, so I don't really recall her being that heavy. It seemed that for years she lived on boiled chicken and lettuce. It worked for her. She now weighs about 160. Being diagnosed with adult onset diabetes was most likely a large component of her motivation.

The apple doesn't fall too far from the tree, though, and most of us have daily struggles with our weight. We do love to eat, and any excuse will do.

"It's raining," one sibling reports.

"Okay, let's eat."

A few days later another says, "The sun is shining."

"Yeah! Let's eat," we respond.

"I went to town today. Got some meat to put on the pit."

"All right, let's eat it up!" No reason needed! Let's eat!

Hunger is never a reliable indicator of when it's time to eat. We don't believe we should get hungry in the first place, bringing

Al, Gus, and Soldum visit around the BBQ pit

all efforts to bear toward the avoidance of that plague—hunger. There have been few occasions when any of us experienced true hunger pangs. The closest most of us have gotten is the attainment of that "slightly less than full" feeling, which to normal folks means that you just ate about an hour ago, but to us means a meal is long overdue and it's way past time to eat again.

In order to fraternize and socialize, and to show our love for each other as well as our love for food, we get together for all major and most minor holidays. No gathering is complete unless there is enough food to feed at least 100 people. Usually there are less than twenty-five of us actually in attendance except for Christmas or Thanksgiving, when the number may swell to about fifty or so, and we all swell with about five additional pounds. Annual homecoming/family reunion may find our numbers way up to about seventy-five—and we "weigh" up to who knows what. We bake, barbeque, fry, fricassee, grill, sauté, and eat raw enough food to feed any of Uncle Sam's armies. It's really something to experience.

As much as I have "gone on" about my family's appetites, you might imagine us as a bunch of over-fed self-indulgents with individual weights equal to that of most grain-fed cattle. We really aren't that huge. We can walk down any Main Street, USA, or into any restaurant and not attract attention. We don't each order everything on the menu, and owners of establishments which serve buffet style do not groan aloud when we walk through the door. The important point to notice here is that I said we *can walk*. We do not have to be rolled, carted, pulled, hoisted, or toted any place. Nor are we a lazy crew, not by any means. Each and every one of us has at least one piece of well-used exercise equipment in our homes. We use the equipment to hang laundry on, prop open doors, hold down loose pieces of paper, etc. One of my sisters uses her gravity climber to hold her hanging begonia plants. They look real nice. Yep! It's well-used stuff.

My siblings and I do try to maintain a semblance of normalcy regarding our size, being aware of the health risks of being overweight and rather vain. Unfortunately for us, we got double zapped with the "fat gene gun." Actually, it's not so much fat as "big." The whole family for generations back simply stand tall and hefty. I like to think it makes us uniquely statuesque.

CHAPTER 12: THE SASSAFRAS EXPEDITION

Being big and tall was an asset in ways other than "gettin' in the crop." We were fearless as youngsters; we'd go anywhere and do anything as long as it was legal (pretty much) and harmless to other people. That adventurous spirit has not diminished in any way with the coming of age and supposed maturity. We still like to know the answer to whatever the prevailing question is. In fact, curiosity is why I went in search of a certain kind of tree just two short years ago at the mature age of thirty-five. The incident with the trees started when Cousin Debbie came by the house one afternoon, asking if I knew what a sassafras tree looked like.

Debbie had recently moved to East Texas from Dallas. I was fairly certain she had not gotten interested in sassafras from any information she'd received in the city. She bore this out, explaining that Cousin Claudia Mae had mentioned the tree to her. Cousin Claudia Mae's description of the tree's properties had intrigued Debbie so much that she decided she wanted to find one.

After a moment's consideration, I recalled that Aunt Jeffie used to make tea from sassafras tree roots. Aunt Jeffie made sassafras tea by boiling the root until the water turned a nice shade of near-fuchsia pink, then adding Carnation milk and sugar to the mixture. I remembered the drink as warm and soothing and rich. I told Debbie that I had indeed heard of sassafras trees but had no idea what one looked like.

With that rekindled memory, I decided to help in the search. I figured the best person to ask where to find these trees would be my mother. When I mentioned that Debbie and I wanted to know what a sassafras tree looked like, I detected a note of whimsy in her reply.

"Well," she answered, "I don't remember what the tree looked like, but there used to be a grove of them right up there in the field."

This spot was easily visible from our kitchen window, so I asked Mama to point out a tree for me. She reminded me that she did not remember what the tree looked like. I would have to go find it for myself.

She did provide this bit of direction. "When you find it you'll know it by the smell." I didn't believe this, but now was not the time to start arguing with Mama.

"What does it smell like?" I asked.

"I can't describe the scent," my mother replied, "but once you smell it, you'll know."

You can imagine how much sense this made to me, but, ever the optimist, I set out to find the trees, arming myself with a shovel, an axe, and that bit of information. I thought that I would first locate a potential subject, sniff the leaves, and peel off some bark; if I still didn't detect this mystery scent, I would use the axe to cut the blame tree down and then use the shovel to dig up some roots.

Off I went.

I headed toward the spot my mother pointed out, soon finding myself in a small copse of young saplings. *Wouldn't it be nice if this was the right place, these the right trees*, I thought to myself. I broke off a low-hanging branch from one of the larger trees, sniffing the bare spot where I had severed it from the trunk of the tree. The aroma was faint but pleasant.

Sure, I had found my tree. I gathered up my tools and headed back down the hill.

I was sorely disappointed when my mother looked at the branch, smelled it, and promptly burst my bubble. "This isn't it." She sounded so sure of herself, while I wondered how she knew. After all, she couldn't even remember what the tree looked like.

I was convinced that this was the right tree and that she just couldn't smell it. By the way, this was the same woman who walked around the kitchen for ten minutes with her terry cloth robe on fire after she'd gotten a bit too close to the gas burner. She didn't smell the smoke, didn't realize she was on fire until she felt the heat on her arms. Mama's sense of smell had been dulled by years of diabetes. Could I trust her to recognize the scent of sassafras? Hmm.

Just to be on the safe side, I asked again, "Well, what does it smell like, then?"

"I can't describe it," she said, "but when you find it you will know."

I'd heard that before.

About that time I heard a car drive up. I went to the front door to see who had come calling. When you live this far back in the woods, any visitor is welcome. It turned out to be sister Maye; she and my mother were going to church that night, and she was there to pick Mom up.

Maye is quite a bit older than I and was sure to have more exacting memories of the smell and physical characteristics of the sassafras tree. I thought I could depend on her to give me the information I needed. Like I said, *I thought. . . .*

I sprightly skipped my way down the four concrete steps, meeting Maye at the gate to the front yard. After a brief "hello" I stated my need, trying to keep my voice calm and nonchalant, letting none of my frustration show. "Do you know about sassafras trees?"

"Why yes, I do. I used to help Papa Charlie dig up roots every fall. We would take a big croaker sack to the grove of sassafras trees that used to be just up the hill there. We'd take the axe and hack at the roots until we had enough to last the winter."

"Last the winter?" I asked.

"Yes, that's what we drank on cold winter evenings."

By now I was so excited I could hardly contain myself. She had not only tasted the tea but had actually helped dig up the roots. There was no way Maye would not be able to help me find these mystical magical trees.

By now, Maye was obviously reminiscing, because she went on and on about how hard it was to dig up those roots.

Yeah! I guess it was hard since she had to have been doing all the hacking and digging by herself. I hope that had been the case, 'cause Papa Charlie was blind as a bat. Blindness doesn't do much for wielding an axe.

I could wait no longer. "What does the tree look like?"

I shouldn't have been so crestfallen with Maye's reply, but I was. "I don't remember what the tree looked like."

Okay. I plunged ahead. "Well, what does it smell like?"

To her credit, Maye at least tried to think of descriptive words—in vain. I was shattered with her next words. "I can't describe it, but you'll know it when you smell it."

I was getting pretty sick of this. I did what I should have done in the beginning.

Cousin Claudia Mae lived about a half-mile or so from us, just across the small creek that ran a few hundred yards south of our house. It took me less than ten minutes to gain access to her living room. After greeting my cousin I got right to the point—so did she.

Here at last was the information I sought. Claudia Mae said that most of the trees that I had walked past to get to her house were sassafras trees. Made me feel bright indeed.

Claudia Mae must have read the incredulous look on my face, because with her next breath she directed her friend Bud to go outside and show me a sassafras tree. Bud found his axe and off we went, going no more than twenty feet before he pointed out several saplings.

"Here's some right here." I didn't want to believe it. No way was this the tree. Bud pulled off a branch, watching my face as I leaned over to smell it.

"Mmm." The fragrance was all I had heard it was—wonderful. I felt as if I had struck gold.

Bud suggested I take the branch with me so I would be able to easily identify the correct tree. I was full of myself now, smugly assured that I would be able to remember the tree's properties, all of them, for the rest of my natural life. I politely declined his offer. Hah!

Bright and early the next morning I got my shovel and axe and headed back to the grove up by the home place, anxious to dig up a few roots for tea. When I got to the grove I was appalled to realize that I had no memory at all about the tree Bud had shown me. I remembered how Maye and Mama had tried vainly to describe sassafras. I was humbled.

I had no choice but to go back to Cousin Claudia Mae's house and prey upon Bud's sympathy, hoping he would take me in hand and guide me to not one but a slew of sassafras trees, enough to imprint their image on my brain forever. Bud laughed when I told him I had forgotten what he had shown me just the evening before.

He cheerfully pointed out the multitude of trees along the fence row, offering me another branch to take with me. Heck, he even offered to dig a whole darn tree. This time I took the proffered branch but declined the offer of the sapling. There were hundreds of sassafras trees right in front of my face; surely I didn't need to take a whole tree along with me.

I left Bud after thanking him profusely and walked the short distance to Debbie's home. As I walked along I realized that the area was indeed full of these trees, which were very easy to find if you knew what you were looking for.

When I saw Debbie, I told her how my search for the tree had gone. Lo and behold, there was a grove of sassafras trees literally in her backyard. She could have reached outside her back door and dug up all the roots she could ever want. I was plumb "got off with." I was even more perturbed when, the next morning, I discovered three trees right beside my parent's mailbox.

Talk about the forest and the trees!

The tea was wonderful, aromatic, and soothing. I drank a lot of it that winter. Sharing the roots with my family sparked memories for us all.

Tenchie and Bubba took bags of the roots back to California with them. Sister Byrd said that when she told her husband Verdell about my "discovery," he remarked that he remembered growing up drinking the tea by the gallon.

"What did you drink it for?" she'd asked him.

I know that what she meant was, "What was the medicinal or recreational purpose for drinking the tea?"

"We drank it to have something to drink," Verdell would reply. It got off with Byrd rather badly, though she was able to laugh about it when she told me the story.

And so it goes.

CHAPTER 13: MAMA AND HER GREEN THUMB

It was not all fun and games back then. We worked very hard helping our parents take care of us. As if there was not enough to do, some folks went so far as to make work. My mother did that—a lot.

Mama was the only woman I have ever known who regularly hauled outside all the beds, bedding, mattresses, springs, bedsteads—everything! She draped the heavy cotton-stuffed mattresses over the fence and lay the springs on the ground. She stood the bedsteads against the trees and shrubs. Mama did all this so that everything could "sun" and "air out." She also had another purpose.

Mama filled her old pump-style sprayer with water and DDT (now banned). She sprayed the bed springs with this mixture to kill bed bugs, spiders, mites, and whatever else lingered near. This toxic chemical probably did not do us much good, either.

Mama believed in DDT. Not only did she use it to spray the metal bed springs, she also used it to sweep down the front porch. She mixed a few ounces into a bucket of hot water and splashed it around on the wooden porch, using a straw broom to get into all the cracks and crevices. This process ridded the area of everything. Every insect known to man could be killed by a DDT cocktail of some ratio or another. No wonder they banned the stuff.

Mama was not always out to kill things. She also had another side. This is not to say she was schizo or anything; she was just a well-rounded woman. She could sew and cook and do all those Mommy things, but she found her true niche the spring she discovered her green thumb.

Mama loved flowers, but there were absolutely none in our yard. Not in front. Not on the sides, in back, or anywhere. One particular spring—I was twelve or so—Mama fell in love with the art and science of horticulture. The front yard was her starting place. The ground was red dirt packed hard as a rock. The ground was so bad that not even weeds grew there. Lots and lots of soil amendment would be needed before the earth would yield anything.

There were cows, hogs, and chickens scattered all over the community, so there was no lack of something to amend the earth with. There was also no shortage of amendees. That would be us, Sister Girl and me. We would be the unfortunate ones charged with the task of amending the soil in our yard.

We did not even have a wheelbarrow to help ease the burden. Sister Girl and I hauled hundreds of pounds of composted cow and chicken manure from the "lot" out back, five gallons at a time. We hauled sh-- until the cows came home. They came home and left more of it for us to haul.

Not only did we not have a wheelbarrow, but the five-gallon containers were made of heavy metal, not plastic as many of them are today. They were heavy all by themselves, and grew considerably heavier with the addition of the manure. The big buckets were originally used to sell and store everything from shortening to axle grease. They were plentiful. We used a bunch of them. If Sister Girl and I were feeling particularly strong in our backs and arms, we doubled up and carried two cans each. The job got done much faster this way, but our backs suffered mightily.

The soil amending never ended. We hauled fifty or sixty pounds of manure after school every day or two. Each time we mistakenly believed we had enough to last the season. To our chagrin, Mama incessantly informed us of her future plans, plans which would require even more manure. She planted and she planted. She bought, borrowed and swapped seeds, cuttings, plants. You name it.

Admittedly, she did have an impressive green thumb. Then again, one's thumb does not have to be much more than pastel green when the soil is good. With all our hard work, the soil was good.

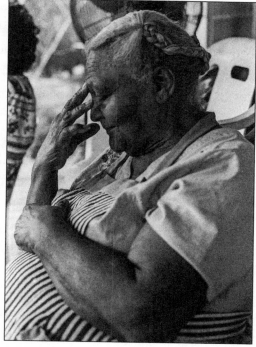

Leota Upshaw

Mama's flowers were beautiful; everyone who drove or walked by commented on her front yard. Before long it was overgrown with flora. It was time to move to the yard on the south side of the house. We dug and we planted, hauled manure, then dug and planted and hauled some more manure. By now Sister Girl and I were sure of it: our mother had finally snapped, gone completely crazy.

We discussed it often: "How can we get her over to Rusk?" we asked ourselves. Rusk was the location of the nearest hospital for the criminally insane.

Interestingly, no one else in the family noticed anything amiss. Neither her husband nor her other children realized that Mama had lost her mind. But then, why should they? They were not the ones hauling the sh--. Sister Girl and I saw no earthly purpose for all these flowers and plants. If there was a heavenly purpose, we were quite sure Mama was a shoo-in for fulfilling it.

If all this planting wasn't enough to break our backs, then the next thing Mama decided to do was destined to finish us off.

During the first winter following her spring-planting-frenzy, Mama realized that although we live in the South, some of her vegetation was not very hardy. The plants would not survive the cold and would need protection. Industrious soul that she was, she straight-away put Sister Girl and me to work digging a pit for her plants. Yes, a pit!

This hole was almost as deep and long as the slush pit the oil workers had used when they were drilling for oil several years before. They had bull dozers and backhoes to do this heavy work for them. We had nothing but our matching shovels and our supple young backs. After several days of hard, back-breaking work, the pit was finished. It was about ten feet by eight feet and approximately six feet deep. It could easily have held six or seven adult-size bodies. I fantasized about filling that pit with the remains of all those good buddies who had given our mother those plants and cuttings, provoking her to lose her mind.

When the first cold snap of autumn came, we were ready. Mama had crafted makeshift shelves for the pit using those same five-gallon cans we had hauled the manure in. She laid 2 × 12s length-wise across the cans. After the shelves were in place we were ready for the next phase.

You guessed it! We dug up all those tender plants. Millions and millions of them, and transplanted them into one- and five-gallon plastic nursery pots before placing them in the pit.

The most tender and least cold-tolerant vegetation was placed on the bottom, directly on the packed dirt floor. The remainder of the plants were layered according to their ability to tolerate cold weather and in accordance with their need for sunlight. After all the plants were in place we laid heavy clear plastic over the pit. There was a wooden frame around the circumference of the pit. We used it to anchor and secure the thick plastic. With the plants safely inside the pit, all we had to do was water them occasionally. If it rained often we did not even have to do that.

The pit-plan was a success. I had kind of hoped that all the plants would freeze to death at the first sign of frost so we would not have to take them out and replant them. No such luck.

Mama lost a few plants—very few! As soon as the weather warmed up we began dragging them all out, transplanting them once more back into the yard. Naturally, the soil had to be amended again. The winter rains had washed away some of the manure incorporated the previous spring.

The next spring and summer passed much like the one before. Mama now knew a little bit more about gardening and was anxious to broaden her horizons to include more delicate and exotic plants.

A little knowledge is a dangerous thing.

Mama loved her flowers, and we begrudged her not one leaf, bud, or petal. We did not mind at all that Mama was so fond of flowers. However, Sister Girl and I agreed that one should not force others to participate in one's hobby. If one wants to plant millions of flowers, then one is welcome to do so. But! One should not expect others to share the enthusiasm with which she approaches the task. Mama forced us to *enthusiastically* assist with her hobby.

After we retrieved and transplanted the flowers the second spring, we began to notice that the pit was considerably smaller than it had been when we first excavated. The rain had eroded the dirt, causing the pit to fill in. We did not use the pit after that year, and not too many seasons later the pit completely disappeared, filled in with mother earth. Good old mother earth! If you looked at the spot now you would never believe it had once been the site of our homemade greenhouse. It is as smooth and level as the rest of the lawn.

All of Mama's attention to her flowers meant that something had to be missing. That something was the vegetable garden. The vegetable plot was Butch's domain, but Mama did help. We all did.

Early each spring Butch did what his forebears had done for generations before him: he hitched his mule to the plow and commenced to turning under the dead foliage of winter. This was known as "breaking up the garden." Once this was done he began to form the rows in neat long lines, which would later be planted and become our winter fodder.

Gardening was serious business. If you did not grow food you would starve. The extended family would ensure that everyone had plenty to eat.

The vegetable garden was located about twenty yards from the back door step. There was an old pear tree in the northwest corner of the plot. I do not know why my parents decided to put the garden right there by that tree. I believe the tree preceded the garden. It had certainly been there for as long as I could remember. I am told it grew from a cutting off of my paternal grandmother's tree.

The pears from the tree were hard and grainy, but not too good for eating. They made excellent preserves, though, if you were into that sort of thing. Incidentally, canning and "putting up" preserves, jellies, and such was another thing I said I would never do.

I said, as I sat there peeling thousands upon thousands of pounds of pears, peaches, etc. for my mother, that if what I wanted to spread on my bread couldn't be bought at the grocery store, I would eat it plain.

Time does bring about a change, however. Now I make the best plum jelly in this part of the country. I also can preserves and vegetables. I guess the apple really does not fall too far from the tree.

Toward the middle of March, after the garden was prepared, we sowed the seeds of cold tolerant, hardy plants. One never knew when the Easter snap was gonna fall or how severe it would be, so it paid to be careful about what you planted early in the season. The cold weather crop included lettuce and other greens and root crops such as carrots. Peas, beans, tomatoes, cucumbers, and the rest were planted a bit later.

Our garden was not overly large. It was a "kitchen garden," the produce used mainly for ourselves. There were several huge fields on the property which were planted in truck farms, their produce meant for market. Fortunately for me, by the time I came along, most truck farming had ceased.

We kids felt the kitchen garden was more than enough to keep us busy. This was our domain—not by choice, mind you, but by design. The design being that if you didn't get out there and work, when and how you were told to, your behind would bear certain designs of its own.

The hardest thing about gardening was watering the young plants. These were the days before advanced irrigating systems (several super long garden hoses strung together) were available to us. Other people had them, I'm sure. We did not. We hauled the water in those infamous, all-purpose five-gallon cans. At least we did not have to carry it by hand. My father, years before, had built a "sled," which we for some unknown reason dubbed a "slide."

We filled the huge cans with water or fertilizer, whatever the need of the day happened to be, and loaded them onto the slide. Sometimes we made two or three trips to get everything we needed to the garden. We did not mind, since we not only enjoyed riding on the slide, but the extra trips delayed the time before we had to begin working in the garden.

We used to wonder among ourselves why Butch didn't just make us kids get off and walk to the garden. He could have hauled everything else in one trip had he made us get off. Maybe Butch was a bit on the lazy side himself . . . ?

The slide was a wooden affair with 2 × 6s forming the boards which moved along the ground. There was a frame of 2 × 4s supporting the 1 × 6s which formed the floor of the slide. An apparatus on the front was hitched to the mule's harness. The 2 × 6s were rounded on the end nearest the mule to facilitate the sliding motion. All in all, it was a very functional tool. It made our work easier and our days in the garden a bit more fun as we savored the rides to and fro.

One afternoon Gus, Pete, Sister Girl, and I were on the slide along with a couple of fifty-pound bags of fertilizer (the kind you buy, not the kind cows make). We sat, tailor-fashion, pretty as you please on the slide. Butch led the mule, walking alongside the animal's head with one of his hands laced through the bridle.

Ole Coley was a gentle soul; all you had to do was give him a general idea of which way you wanted him to go and he'd do you proud. Actually, once he was hitched up to the slide, Ole Coley knew we were going to the garden. I think Butch had his hand in the bridle as a way to rest his weary arm rather than to guide the mule.

There we were, riding along, laughing and talking, no doubt discussing State secrets. I cannot recall which ones. What I do remember is what happened when the slide hit a bump.

It was not a big bump, just enough to dislodge Sister Girl from her seat. What happened next was truly amazing. That she fell off the slide was unspectacular. What was truly amazing was the way the slide ran over her.

Because she was sitting toward the front of the slide, Sister Girl landed just behind the mule's feet when she landed. This all happened so swiftly that no one could react.

There was Butch, ambling along beside Ole Coley and resting his hand in Coley's bridle. He didn't even know what had happened until it was all over (but the shouting).

Sister Girl fell. The slide kept moving. Coley and Butch never broke stride as the slide slid right over her. Pete, Gus, and I watched in awe as we waited for Sister Girl's body to emerge from the back end of the conveyance. There was a considerable bump-bump-bump as the slide moved over her chubby body. Within a second or two (an eternity if you happened to be the one underneath the slide) there she was.

The slide moved off her and left her lying there in the soft, sandy loam. The most stupefying fact of all was that Sister Girl was not injured.

She was dirty and dusty, but she was that way before she fell off. There may have been one or two minor scrapes somewhere on her hide, but that was all. Considering that approximately four hundred pounds of fertilizer and human beings had just been dragged over her, Sister Girl emerged from under the slide appearing quite fit.

By the time the slide was going "bump, bump" the rest of us kids had found our voices.

"Missonnell, Missonnell!" we all shouted, hollering at the top of our lungs even though Butch was less than six feet from us.

Detecting the note of terror in our voices, Butch quickly reined in Ole Coley, "Whoa, boy!" he said. Coley must have sensed that Butch was serious, because he stopped dead in his tracks and stood stock still as Butch eased his hand from the bridle.

"You ran over Sister Girl!" we exclaimed as Butch hurriedly walked the short distance to the slide. I guess he thought his expensive fertilizer had fallen off. He did not at first notice that he had a child missing.

"You ran over Sister Girl," we repeated when it became apparent that Butch had no clue what was wrong. His fertilizer was all there, after all, safe and sound on the slide just where he had placed it.

It really wasn't Butch's fault that Sister Girl fell. Well, only so far as he was driving.

Ole Coley came to a complete stop, helped along by a firm tug on his bridle and that no-nonsense "Whoa!" from Butch. We jumped off the slide and rushed the ten or so feet to where Sister Girl still lay in the dirt. We looked closely for signs of death or at least severe injury.

Our fallen comrade lay inert for a moment, but we soon saw life. She had not been killed after all. There were no bones or bone fragments sticking out anywhere. No scattered appendages littering the field. Her head was not busted open, no brains oozed from her ears or nose. She did not even bleed.

It took us about ten seconds to determine that Sister Girl was just fine. Then, the humor of the situation struck us. We sized up the hilarity of the experience and began to roar with laughter.

Yes, this was our sister and daughter, but . . . excitement is excitement. We took it where we could get it. She could have at least had the grace to bleed a little. Since she wasn't hurt we felt she deserved to be laughed at. She had fallen off a slide, for goodness sake. The slide was less than a foot off the ground. How does one fall off something that close to the earth? I guess it was akin to falling off a log.

Anyway, we felt no guilt about laughing. She would have done the same for us. We helped Sister Girl to her feet, dusted her off, and hopped back on the slide. Sister Girl sat toward the back from that point onward.

Moments later Gus, Pete, and I were teasing Sister Girl about how that fall had "plumb scared the color off her." The off-white sandy dirt had left Sister Girl a much paler hue, from her hair all the way down to her bare toes.

****

I hated gardening. I swore that, once I grew up, I would never plant a thing, nothing. I vowed I'd get all my produce from the place where you're supposed to get it—the grocery store. If the store didn't have it, I would do without. I did not care for flowers, either. Nice, green grass was good enough for me. Only the freshly dead needed flowers. And they did not really need them.

I kept that vow for years, the itch not catching up with me until about ten years ago. I looked down at my hands one fine spring day and noticed with horror. My thumbs were turning green!

Guess what I do for a hobby now.

CHAPTER 14: SISTER GIRL AND THE SNAKE

The only person I know who hates snakes more than I do is my sister Byrd. Her favorite expression on the subject—"I hate a snake"—is a sentiment I quite agree with. There are those who espouse the benefits that snakes bring to our ecological balance. Fine. My personal belief is that the only good snake is a dead snake. I fear them. I despise them. Not everyone in my family feels such high levels of animosity toward those slithering examples of God's wrath. There is Sister Girl. She may feel disdain for snakes, but she apparently is not afraid of them.

One day, Faye and Byrd were outside raking leaves. A big snake happened by and they killed it.

Faye and Byrd beat the snake until his battered and bruised head resembled the red dirt he was bleeding into. They were proud of their accomplishment and rightfully so. Showing off your quarry was one of the joys of killing snakes.

Everyone who saw it remarked about its impressive size. Some speculated as to why such a large snake happened to be in the road. Others commented on its genus and species. Genus and species were unimportant. The overall "snake" category was sufficient to mark the varmint as the enemy.

After Byrd and Faye killed the unfortunate critter they dragged him back into the yard using the tines of the same rake that they had just used the tail of to annihilate him with. They stretched the snake out to its full impressive length. He was a big snake, a big dead snake. That snake was undoubtedly right then giving an account of himself before his maker.

"What about that mouse you ate when you were already full?" his Maker asks, and, "What about that lady you bit after she was kind enough to feed and house you?" A snake has no shame and thus, his answer would invariably be, "She knowed I was a snake." I digress.

The snake lay relatively still for quite some time. There was an occasional twitch and an infrequent semi-slither. Snakes are notorious for their "bad nerves"; they keep twitching for hours after they're supposed to be dead. Snake nerves are like Eveready batteries—they keep going and going and going. I personally don't trust a snake until I can see his skeletal remains. Then I know for certain. He's dead!

After the snake thrashing, Faye and Byrd went back to their yard cleaning, all but forgetting the snake. Sister Girl didn't forget about him, though. She decided to really let that snake know just how low she thought he was.

Our sister sidled close to the snake, watching closely to ensure his "late" state. After ascertaining that the snake had passed on, Sister Girl squatted down and began to pee on the snake's afore-mentioned battered and bruised head.

Miss Girl obviously wasn't paying attention to what else was going on in her world, concentrating as she was on producing a nice steady stream of pee. Sister Girl had only been urinating a few seconds when she heard Faye's warning.

"Watch out, Sister Girl!" Faye shouted at the top of her soprano voice. Sister Girl jumped up and looked down in time to witness the snake rearing his ugly head, straight up toward her butt.

So! He wasn't quite dead after all. Sister Girl was stunned, rendered speechless by her close call with a snake bite. We, on the other hand, wondered if there was something magical about Sister Girl's pee. Did it have resurrecting qualities?

We probably missed our opportunity to make billions of dollars by not calling Ciba-Geigy or Dow Chemical that day. I don't imagine Sister Girl's pee has retained the quality to raise the dead. She and it are older now and less pure than in those days. That experience taught Miss Girl a valuable lesson about when you "assume." Not only might it make an "ass" out of "u" and "me," it might also cause you to get your ass bitten.

Snakes weren't the only varmints we had to contend with back in the olden days. The woods were full of wild animals. There were coyotes—lots of them—bobcats, brown bear, and so on. Uncle N. E. maintained there were panthers in the woods as well. He said when he hunted at night he sometimes heard those cats screaming and howling. He claimed that they sounded just like a woman screaming.

Panthers and bears! Oh my. I never saw any, but I have seen coyotes and bobcats. I also know about rabid dogs. Now, there's something to be scared of! Forget haunts and ghosts and such. Rabid dogs were a real and present danger.

Every now and then the men in community had to mobilize themselves to hunt down a rabid animal. Domesticated or feral, it did not matter. If the animal were rabid, the men hunted him until they found and destroyed him.

One of the dogs that contracted rabies belonged to us. We were unsure how the dog caught the disease . . . there's just no telling. The dogs in the area were all allowed to roam freely, so it is likely our pet got rabies from a wild animal rather than from a domestic one.

Murphy had been a part of our family for several years, coming to us as a puppy. He was a mongrel, friendly and playful by nature. We were very fond of him. Our close association with the animal ended abruptly when he came down with rabies. There is no room for sentiment when dealing with such an illness.

When we saw the animal after he'd gotten rabies, we knew immediately that something was very wrong with him. He snarled and snapped at us. His playful nature was gone forever.

It was a Saturday morning and we kids had completed most of our chores for the day. With the work done we were free to watch an hour or two of cartoons on our old black and white RCA.

Our R & R was interrupted by a call informing us that there was a rabid dog on the loose. We had no idea it was our dog.

Mama took the call in the kitchen. Before she walked into the living room where we sat watching television we knew the facts ourselves.

Someone had left the front door open. It was a nice day outside and opening the door was a common practice. There was no reason not to, except for the fact that a crazed animal roamed the area. However, we did not know it at the time.

We heard him growling and snarling even before Murphy jumped upon the porch. Mama had just entered the room, planning to tell us about the rabid dog. There was no time to warn us. The dog was already in the house.

Murphy ran around and around the living room while we stood, a petrified knot on the sofa.

When the dog ran into the room all we had time to do was jump, as a unit, onto the couch. We three stood there clinging to each other, scared out of our wits. Murphy had the look of a lunatic. His mouth dripped deadly saliva as he slung his head from side to side. His eyes were glazed and he was frantic. So were we.

Mama wasted no time. If even a small drop of saliva made contact with an open place on our bodies, we, too would become stricken with rabies, destined to suffer just as the mad dog before us. She knew this and so did we. Mama grabbed the first thing her hand reached, a broom. Fortunately, the broom was very sturdy with a thick, strong handle. Mama began brandishing the makeshift weapon like a wild woman. She swung the broom handle at Murphy, prodding him slowly but surely back to the front door. She yelled and pushed, poked and pummeled until the dog finally retreated.

We were too young to realize it, but Mama was more frightened than we were. We had only heard a little about what rabies would do to you. Most of the information we got was from television, fictional westerns mostly. Mama had seen its effects firsthand when a cousin of hers contracted the disease. All we knew was that our Mama beat the daylights out of that dog.

As she almost always did when it was her up against an animal, Mama won. She got the dog out of the house. She did not kill him, but he was so battered that when the men drove up a few minutes later they were able to easily catch up with the animal. Sadly, the men who had been hunting the dog had to shoot him, putting him out of his misery and us all out of danger.

After the dog was out of the house, Mama set about cleaning the room and the front porch. She shooed us out the back door, admonishing us to go no further. She gathered up cleaning materials: bleach, Tide, pine oil cleanser, and a five-gallon bucket of very hot water. Mama used her stiff cleaning brush to wash, vigorously swirling the solution all over the hardwood floor. She scrubbed and scrubbed until she was satisfied that there was no danger from errant germs. After the living room was clean, Mama repeated the procedure on the front porch. When she finished both areas could have served as surgical arenas, they were so antiseptic.

It only took Mama a few minutes to eradicate all possible germs. It was years before I realized that she did what was necessary to protect us from rabies by washing down the floor. She also worked off nervous energy, using up the excess adrenaline left over after saving our hides—again. Mama never admitted being scared for us. She was, though. Mama had more than that one occasion to be afraid for one or more of us. Looking back, I don't see why she didn't die young from the sheer stress of worrying about all of us.

Then again, I *do* know. She had a lot of help looking out for us. Her prayers, and the prayers of forebears from ages past were sufficient to keep us in His care. That was all we ever needed.

CHAPTER 15: AUNT ANNIE BELL

One of the sweetest, kindest folks I ever knew was our Aunt Annie Bell. She lived about a hundred yards from us on the old home place. Her house was well within hollering of our home so we were free to visit as often as we wished. In a sense, Auntie's was "neutral" territory, a place where everyone felt comfortable and safe. Every Sunday afternoon, Aunt Jeffie and the girls of the "famous five" would come down to Auntie's to sit a spell. A "spell" usually lasted about three hours. That span of time was never enough for us kids, so we always begged Aunt Jeffie to stay a while longer. When that "while" passed, we begged some more. Often our pleas were effective, and we had a little extra time to play.

There was a huge ancient oak tree just in the curve of the road in front of the home place. We played for hours underneath that old oak. The road continues past our house. From the porch we had an unrestricted view of the road and could see all the traffic to and from Auntie's and Uncle Floyd's homes.

The Old Home Place, where Monel and Leota lived and raised their children

Whenever Sister Girl or I saw Aunt Jeffie's Chevy pickup truck, we would ask Mama for permission to go to Auntie's to play. Once there we played for hours, whiling the afternoon away under that big tree. It didn't bother us that we were playing in the middle of the road. We could hear the cars coming—if there were any. The middle of the road was about as safe as anywhere else. Once, though, a car somehow sneaked up on us. It was not deliberate. The driver had no idea we were in the road. Reverend D'Effie drove so slowly that his car's engine was virtually silent. We simply did not hear it approaching.

We girls were playing hopscotch underneath the tree when Jeffie Mae decided she needed to use the bathroom. She didn't want to walk back to Auntie's house, and she saw no reason to hide behind the tree. She was going to pee. Then and there.

After peeping around the curve to ensure that no cars were coming, Jeffie Mae squatted in the road. She chose the middle of the road because she wanted (and wanted us) to watch her urine flow down the incline. I guess she wanted to see how far it would travel before soaking into the hot dust of the road.

Jeffie Mae peed and we kept playing. We weren't particularly interested in Jeffie Mae's urine or its flow pattern. We had seen it all before. Unfortunately for Jeffie Mae, our loud raucous laughter kept us from hearing Rev. D'Effie's car as it approached the curve.

Jeffie Mae looked up just in time to spot Rev. D'Effie spotting her. She stood up quick as lightning her pee freezing in midstream. Her bladder was suddenly so paralyzed that it was days before she could urinate freely again.

She was embarrassed. Jeffie Mae had been caught with her pants down, pissing, and by the preacher, no less. None of us had ever gotten caught peeing outside before. The rest of us thought it outrageously funny that Jeffie had gotten caught like that. She laughed along with us but I doubt she found it as amusing as we did.

We did lots of silly things at Auntie's house, but we also played regular "little girl" games. The sandy loam in front of the home is where we learned to play hopscotch, Mary Mack, ring-around-the-rosie and so forth. It was where we discussed our hopes and dreams for the future and shared our fantasies about the present. They were good days. The times spent at the home place and out under that old oak tree are among the best I can remember.

Our hostess, Aunt Annie Bell, had been married once upon a time. Her married name was Annie Bell Sparks. We always knew her as Annie Bell Upshaw. I never knew what happened to that husband. He was gone years before I was born.

Funny thing about husbands—none of my three aunts had one. They all had had one at some point, but not for many, many years. The brothers were all married except for Uncle Hadie, but the sisters were widowed, divorced—alone. Interestingly, two of the sisters, Aunt LA and Aunt Jeffie, had married brothers. Both preceded their wives in death by decades.

By the time I knew her, Aunt Annie Bell and our Cousin Charlie Bailey lived together. Not in a romantic sense. They just lived together. It was that way all my life. The only significance of this fact is that it demonstrates the way kin folks took care of and looked out for each other back then.

Both Auntie and Cousin Charlie were blind. Neither of them could see a hand in front of their faces. If that weren't bad enough, Aunt Annie Bell had lost a leg (just above the knee) as well as her eyesight to diabetes. I never knew what caused Cousin Charlie's blindness.

When I was in elementary school and just learning to read, I used to go up to Auntie's to show off my budding academic prowess. I'm sure she must have been bored to tears with my pitiful renditions of Dick and Jane. I am sure also that she was familiar enough with the story to know when I was reading correctly and when I was embellishing the story. In any case, she always listened attentively and made appropriate comments as I stumbled along. Aunt Annie Bell was nobody's dummy, having been an educator in her younger years. She knew how to fan my sparked interest in the written word. I appreciated and benefitted from her encouragement. She and Cousin Charlie were inspirations to everyone who knew them, keeping the faith and never complaining or grumbling about their afflictions.

Auntie was deeply religious, though not one to spout off about it. I just always knew that she was. She occasionally came to church, particularly on major occasions like the all-night singing or homecoming Sunday. Her physical infirmities prevented frequent excursions, but she came when she could.

Someone, usually Butch and Uncle N. E., would load Auntie into the car. Aunt Annie Bell had a wheelchair. It was just like one from an Alfred Hitchcock movie. It was large and extremely cumbersome, so she rarely used it. She was carried by her brothers from place to place. They carried her to the car when it was time for church, but they did not bring her into the building. There were several steps leading to the front door, and it would have been difficult to safely carry Auntie inside. As far as I can remember she never came inside the church, but instead remained outside in the car. The windows of the church were open and the car was parked right underneath them. From that vantage point, Aunt Annie Bell could hear everything that went on inside the sanctuary. She got "happy" sometimes, too. We often heard her shouting and clapping her hands. She enjoyed herself immensely, and we enjoyed having her at church even though she was not inside the building with us.

The church had no sound system back then. The amplification the preacher achieved depended strictly on the size of his mouth and the strength of his lungs. I suppose religious zeal also influenced the volume of his delivery. In any case, I never had a doubt that Aunt Annie Bell heard everything that went on inside the church. She could hear exceptionally well. In fact, her hearing seemed to strongly compensate for her visual deficits.

My sister Maye tells this story about Auntie's hearing.

Several of my siblings were visiting Auntie and Cousin Charlie late one afternoon. They were sitting around talking, swapping gossip and telling lies when Auntie broke in.

"I hear somebody crying," she said. "Who is that crying?"

Everyone stopped talking and listened. They heard nothing. Conversation resumed. Auntie interjected again, and then again. Several times she exclaimed that she *knew* she was hearing someone crying. Still, no one else heard anything. This began to make everyone a bit uneasy. If Auntie said she heard somebody crying, then somebody somewhere was crying. Everyone knew Auntie had exceptionally sharp hearing. The group grew quiet as everyone strained to hear. They heard nothing unusual, but just minutes later Cousin Evie Lois walked into their line of vision. When she got to the porch she related tragic news. She told the group that Cousin Laura's son, Arthur Lee, had attempted suicide at his home in West Texas. Apparently distraught over a relationship gone amuck, he had put a gun in his mouth and tried to end his life.

He did not die, fortunately, but the injury left him disfigured. As children, we never paid any attention to the way Cousin Arthur Lee looked. We younger children were not old enough to remember him looking any other way. To us, Cousin Arthur Lee always looked the same and we never thought anything of it. It meant nothing to us. He was kind and generous, and that was all that mattered.

As I grew older I began to realize that while we were growing up our community was filled with people that others might call handicapped or "differently abled," whatever the current politically correct phrase is.

There was Cousin Arthur Lee with his disfigurement. He lived with another cousin, Rufus Bailey, who was closely related to Cousin Charlie Bailey. Cousin Rufus (Rufe) had apparently suffered from some disease or accident which permanently bent him forward at the waist. He also had a large hump in his upper back. I never saw him without his walking stick, and, on top of all that, he was also an unusually small man.

Of course, I have already mentioned that Auntie Annie Bell was a blind amputee.

Uncle Claude and Uncle Hadie both walked with two sticks apiece. They were also humped over, but in a very different way from Cousin Rufus. Rheumatism caused them to bend from the hip rather than the waist. Cousin Rufe had kyphosis. At that time we thought nothing of it, certainly never considered that the condition might actually have a medical name. He was simply Cousin Rufe who had a humped back and walked with a cane. Slowly. We paid his odd appearance no attention except to remark how much Cousin Rufe resembled a turtle. A turtle with a walking stick.

Uncle Claude and Uncle Hadie, later called Uncle Bear and Monel, also suffered from a mild form of spinal bifida. It was probably this, and not the rheumatism, which so severely limited their mobility.

Cousin Rufe and Cousin Arthur Lee both lived with Cousin Li'l Laura Upshaw (Arthur Lee's mother). Cousin "Lar," as we called her, was a tiny, *tiny* wizened old woman with a face like a prune. I mean just like a prune, both black and wrinkled. We did not find this odd. Cousin Lar had a twin sister who lived in a neighboring community. Whenever the twin visited we kids would stare in amazement. There they were! Two tiny, wizened, wrinkled little prune ladies. They were quite a spectacle, but two sweeter prunes never lived.

It was past Cousin Lar's house we walked when we short-cut to the store. Right through her yard we went. She did not seem to mind. Nor did she mind when one of my brothers (Gene) decided to detour into the house for a snack.

Cousin Lar was out back tending the livestock when Gene sneaked, or thought he was sneaking, into the house and helped himself to a plate of Cousin Lar's freshly cooked dinner. As he sat there calmly eating, Cousin Lar, who knew all along what he was doing, hollered out, "Don't you eat up all that chicken, Rufe boy."

Gene responded without missing a lick (of his fingers). "Yessum." He kept on eating. When he finished, Gene got up, washed his plate and left, calling out a "thank you" as he passed the livestock lot. Where else but the country!?

It seemed that everyone in the community had a sense of humor, and Uncle Claude was no exception. Every now and then he would amuse us by dancing on his sticks. He was very entertaining, but he was tight with his money. He would give you the shirt off his back, let you sit up in his warm cozy store all day long, telling tall tales beside his old wood heater. He would feed you until you wanted no more. But you needn't ask him to give you any money. *That* he did not do!

Sitting around the store was the favored pastime for the entire community. When it was hot outside, we sat on the homemade wooden benches, chairs, steps, or whatever we could find out on my uncle's porch. We listened to "haint" stories, gossip, whatever was going on. Several of the menfolk always sat on a particular bench. This was their seat, and if any of them were present everybody else kept off. Period! The seat was about five feet long, two-and-a-half feet deep, really quite comfortable. It was a wooden affair hand-crafted of pine planks, which probably started out as

Brother N. E. and Monel Upshaw

rough-cut lumber, but long since worn smooth by all those ample behinds rubbing along its length.

My uncles, Hadie, Floyd and N. E., usually occupied the bench. If Uncle Claude or my father was around, one or the other of them would take the place of whichever of "his highnesses" was absent. There were cousins around all the time, too, who were occasionally allowed to reign—briefly—on the throne. In fact, it was a cousin who told the monarchs off about their bench.

It seems one of the usual sitters was absent, His Royal Highness N. E., I believe. In N. E.'s absence someone suggested to Jessie Morrisette (Aunt LA's roommate) that he should go ahead and sit on the bench since HRH N. E. was absent.

Mr. Morrisette stuttered badly, especially when he got tickled and he, on this occasion, was very tickled. Here, finally, was his chance to "get off" with those "His Royal Highness-Old Buzzards."

"N-n-n-n-n-o-o, I-I-I, ain't go, go-n, g-o-o-o-n-n-n-n-a-a, gonna s-sit on th-tha, that da-da-da bench," Mr. Morrisette sputtered. "T-that's t-the dead pecker bench!"

The men were so outdone they were speechless. Uncle Hadie recovered first and began to roll with laughter. His ample belly heaved and pitched as he chortled. The rest of the fellows soon joined in. Mr. Morrisette had scored—big time with his mangled comment that only men with "dead peckers" sat on that particular bench.

It stood to reason that Uncle Hadie would be the one to recover first from the insult; he was always a bit radical. For instance, he had never married, although he had fathered several children. Fathering children really has nothing to do with marriage, but it did add to his reputation as a maverick. Uncle Hadie was more than a little bit different, not different in any "queer" way, just . . . different. These days whenever there is a long-term bachelor in the family, he can use as his excuse for not marrying, "Well, somebody's got to be like Uncle Hadie."

There are even a few females in the family who have chosen (or had it chosen for them) not to wed. "Lady Hadies" we call them.

Uncle Hadie not only never married, he never really lived with anyone either. He liked his solitude, always lived by himself. This suited his nature, but it branded him a hermit for those who did not know better. No indeed, he was really a sociable guy and often visited others in the community. He would sit and chat with his siblings for a spell. When evening came he headed back to his house, one of several he owned.

CHAPTER 16: UNCLE HADIE'S HOUSES

His habitats were part of what made Uncle Hadie so interesting. He had several houses during the course of his lifetime. Seems something was always happening to Uncle Hadie's houses. The first incident involved an act of nature. From there—who knows?

Uncle Hadie's place was right up the road from our home, just over a quarter mile away. In both winter and summer our East Texas weather is, at best, unpredictable. At worst, it is dangerous. A big storm blew up one late spring afternoon with heavy rain and moderately strong straight-line winds. The gregarious Hadie was visiting his brother, N. E., at the time and decided, wisely, to stay put until the storm had passed. I say "wisely" because after the storm quieted, Uncle Hadie made his way around the corner to his home.

He was seeing things!

As Uncle Hadie approached the area where his house should have been, he discovered quite a sight indeed. The wind had blown Uncle Hadie's house slap over. The building was still right there on the property. It just didn't look the same, lying as it was on the ground. It was definitely not as Hadie had left it. The house had been leaning in the first place, so it should not have been too much of a surprise when it was blown over. The converse is true as well. Since the house had been listing for years, there was no reason to believe it in danger of imminently falling over.

Apparently, the house took on animate qualities. Of its own volition it grew tired, gave up and lay down, yielding to the fierce winds of the storm. The house was finally at peace. When Uncle Hadie beheld the mess of twisted lumber and broken furniture, he was appalled. His house had fallen over!

Houses burned down, Hadie would learn later. They got caught up in tornadoes. Uninhabited homes deteriorate swiftly over what seems like mere weeks, railing against desertion by absent owners. Mice and roaches moved into houses, snakes crawled underneath them. Roofs of houses sprang leaks, paint peeled from the walls inside and out. Timbers rotted and eventually crumbled. Lots of bad things happened to houses.

Houses do not, however, just fall over. No one had ever seen or heard tell of such a thing.

Uncle Hadie was understandably upset. He did not remain so. You can't keep a good man down. He quickly gathered his wits about him and set about constructing a plan, no longer disturbed by the disaster which had struck his house.

Uncle Hadie had several options. He was not a poor man, and he was blessed with lots of family. What he felt he needed, though, was expediency, having no desire to remain homeless one moment longer than necessary. So . . . he set up housekeeping . . . in the potato house.

The potato house had been built years before as a cool dry place to store, you guessed it, potatoes. It kept the tubers in a favorable environment as they cured. The house was also used to store onions and carrots, radishes and turnips, any root vegetable requiring a period of seasoning. The house was about ten feet long by eight feet wide. There was a tin roof over the structure standing about five feet off the ground. Concrete wooden steps led down into the pit about eight feet into the ground. Vented cantilevered metal shelves and steel hooks were intermittently placed along the walls of the structure. The shelves held the curing vegetables. Huge bags of onions swung from steel hooks imbedded in the ceiling rafters.

It was very sturdily built. Certainly it was not going to blow over in a wind storm. The house was very comfortable . . . for potatoes. It was not meant for housing people, but it served in that capacity as well.

The potato house was private, secluded, well-built, and available. As far as Hadie was concerned it was perfect, for the short haul at least. He never intended to spend all his time in the potato house; Uncle Hadie went someplace every day. Daily, he walked the quarter mile to the store where he spent several hours with his brother Claude.

After catching up on the latest gossip and perhaps grabbing a few winks—sleeping on Uncle Claude's porch with his back and head resting on an overturned ladder back chair—Hadie headed to Uncle N. E.'s home. He stayed there a few more hours, often taking his evening meal with them. About dusk-dark Uncle Hadie returned to his potato shed, ready to settle in for the evening.

Hadie had a voracious appetite for reading. He was intelligent and quick-witted as well as well-read. Even in less than ideal circumstances, Hadie read. There was no electricity in the potato house, but Uncle Hadie was undaunted. He was accustomed to reading every evening and had no intention of stopping. He would have to be creative.

The day after his home blew over, Uncle Hadie took a trip to town with one of his brothers, heading straight to the Lone Star Farm and Ranch store. Uncle Hadie purchased a Coleman kerosene lantern and a heavy-duty flashlight. With sufficient reading lighting assured, he was set. Hadie read by the light of his coal oil lantern just about every evening. He wrapped one arm and then the other around the base of the lantern alternately, using his free hand to hold his reading material.

The potato house was small and snug, the earth providing excellent insulation. The oil lantern was enough to keep the room both warm and well illuminated. It is a wonder, though, that he did not burn himself up, baking himself as well as the potatoes.

Uncle Hadie lived like that for about six months. He spent from early spring to the beginning of the following autumn in the earth-beamed structure. By then his new house was complete and he moved out. He lived in his new home for many years, though he would suffer more losses.

We were at Sunday school when Uncle Hadie's new house (well, it wasn't new any longer) caught fire and burned to the ground. He was homeless once again! This time there was no potato pit to serve as a temporary abode. The potato house had long since been filled in and covered over. After Hadie stopped using the structure, it had become a haven for snakes and venomous spiders, so the brothers tore the walls down and filled the hole with dirt. The situation looked grave for the man who so loved his freedom. You can't keep a good man down, though. Remember that.

This time, there was a Plymouth.

Uncle Hadie had bought a thoroughly used car a year or so before the house fire. He had driven it once or twice before it quit for good. It had not been a mechanically sound vehicle, but it was big. Very big. This car was made the way they used to do it, big enough to haul—and perhaps even house—a family.

My other uncles could hardly believe that Hadie was planning to set up housekeeping in the Plymouth. They tried to discourage him, but he was determined to have his own place—immediately. Since they couldn't talk him out of it, the brothers set about making Hadie's new home as comfortable as possible.

Uncle N. E. and one of his boys pulled the seats and the dashboard out of the Plymouth, yielding quite a bit of room. Butch gave Hadie an old, cotton-filled mattress which laid on the car's floor. He added a few cans of sardines and a box of crackers, a bottle of water and some toilet paper, and Uncle Hadie was set once again.

In truth Hadie spent little time in the car, sleeping at our house most evenings and visiting everywhere else during the day. He didn't have to sleep in the car at all . . . ever, and he knew it. He was welcome at any home in the community, but he had to have his space. Uncle Hadie had the car modified and outfitted just so he could have a place to call his own. It did not matter that his place was a car; it was his place; it would do for the "short haul."

Within months Uncle Hadie had a new house. He bought the old community club house and had it moved to his home site. The club house had not been used for many years so he got it very cheaply. As soon as the house was properly set up, my uncle began housekeeping all over again. He bought some necessities, borrowed some others, and received many more as gifts.

The building had been the location for quilting bees and such. The women hadn't quilted there for years (another story) and the house was empty. Selling it to Uncle Hadie worked out nicely. The frame structure originally belonged to my godmother and name-sake Beatrice Hooper. She and Inez Blakey taught school for years in the community's one-room school. The women often spent the night in County Line rather than making the twenty-two-mile trek to their homes in Nacogdoches. The house was used for this purpose.

Our community school eventually merged with a larger district. Mrs. Blakey and Mrs. Hooper began teaching school at other locations, and their vacation home became the club house. My mother and her compadres quilted and sewed at the club house for years. Some of my fondest memories are of playing underneath the quilts as the women stitched above my head.

There must have been something wrong with that particular plot of land. Perhaps it had a history as an ancient burial ground. There had to have been something amiss, because a few years after Uncle Hadie died, this house, too, caught fire and burned to the ground.

Someone was renting the house at the time, and the fire blazed when the tenant foolishly started a fire in the old wood heater using gasoline. I don't imagine he intended to get quite that warm! Uncle Hadie probably spun in his grave, swiftly root-tilling the soil at the Stonewall-Douglass cemetery, where he was housed.

He was a different sort of fellow, but no matter where or how Uncle Hadie lived, he was still very highly thought of, a sport of a guy if there ever was one. He cared deeply for his siblings, often visiting even Aunt Annie Bell, which was a long walk for his crippled legs. He whiled away many an hour with his sister and cousin. I was fortunate enough to hear many a laugh pass between them.

As used to be so common in the country, everybody was willing to help everybody else. This goodwill extended far beyond the occasional visit. If someone needed help only once a year or once in a lifetime, they got it. If someone needed help every day, they got it.

Aunt Annie Bell and Cousin Charlie naturally needed a bit more help than most, since they were both blind. As children we never really thought much about how Auntie and Cousin Charlie managed. I myself made countless treks to their home, taking food or other necessities. Although I did help them often, I certainly didn't help them every day, nor did I help them do everything.

I never wondered who helped Auntie get up every morning, get dressed and get into the orange rocking chair she sat in all day. All I knew was that whenever I saw her, that's where she was sitting, and she was always dressed and groomed for the day.

Auntie had an old wheel chair, the kind with the high wooden back that you only see in Alfred Hitchcock-type movies (moving by itself). I don't recall ever seeing her in the wheel chair. She preferred the old orange rocker. Sometimes she sat outside, if the weather was nice.

It astounds me now that I never once considered how she got to the porch.

Much later, after Auntie died (I was nine years old at the time), I found out that my father and his siblings were the ones who got her up every morning. They helped her dress and took care of the house, chores I had given no thought to.

The pair, my aunt and cousin, were not helpless by any means. Cousin Charlie used to cook even after he lost his sight. Word has it he was pretty good at it. He stopped cooking, though, after accidentally mis-mixing a batch of cornmeal.

Cousin Charlie had planned to make cornbread. He set out the utensils and ingredients and mixed the batter. He had done it a hundred times. This time, though, he mistook a bag of sulfur for the cornmeal.

I bet Aunt Jemima was outdone. How could anyone, blind, crippled or crazy mistake sulfur for cornmeal? The smell should have been a clue. I thought that the loss of one sensory ability caused the others to sharpen. But no one ever said that you could not lose two senses.

Cousin Charlie obviously smelled about as well as he saw. Let me rephrase that. Cousin Charlie could not smell any better than he could see. Let me try again. Cousin Charlie obviously could neither see nor smell. You get the picture. Cousin Charlie's sense of smell was just as impaired as his sense of sight, and he couldn't see his hand in front of his face.

Go figure.

Sulfur has such a potent smell (especially when heated) that one has to be sensorially deficient not to realize that it is different from cornmeal. Somehow, Cousin Charlie made that error. He didn't even catch on until he tasted the cornbread. Oh, well. At least there was nothing wrong with his sense of taste.

It really is hard to believe that someone who cooked regularly could make such a mistake. It was not entirely Charlie's fault, however. Someone else had inadvertently stored the sulfur where the cornmeal should have been. Sulfur was used for a variety of purposes in the days "pre-Raid." It's great for getting rid of insects, snakes, and what-have-you.

After that incident, he never cooked anymore. For him to do it for as long as he did with his infirmity is commendable. After all, we're not talking about going into the kitchen and turning on the stove. We're talking about going out to the woodpile, gathering up kindling, coming back inside and building a fire. That makes it a whole new ball of wax.

CHAPTER 17: CHEE-CHEE AND CHARLIE

After Aunt Annie Bell died back in 1971, her erstwhile room-mate Cousin Charlie moved in with Aunt LA and Mr. Morrisette. Mr. Morrisette had lived with Aunt LA for years, and I never knew why exactly. I do not believe he was closely related to us, nor can I imagine him romantically linked with my aunt.

Frankly, not only did I never know why, I never cared why either. It was most likely a case of him needing a place to live and her needing the company.

As the trio, LA, Charlie and Mr. Morrisette began to age and decline, they more and more frequently missed church. They continued faithfully in their financial support of the church, however, never failing to send their donations by someone. My cousin and running buddy Chee-Chee and I soon got into the habit of walking the hundred yards or so from the church to Auntie's house every Sunday morning to collect their money for the collection.

As soon as Sunday school superintendent Monel Upshaw rang the bell to end class, Chee-Chee and I headed to Aunt LA's house. Usually, we greeted the old folks and collected the money without incident. As is always the case in my family, "usual" is never good enough for long.

We had just been dismissed from Sunday school, but Chee-Chee obviously had the devil in her.

We collected Auntie's money first, then moved on to Mr. Morrisette. Next, we went into Cousin Charlie's bedroom and explained that we were there to pick up his donation. The lights were turned off and the shades were drawn, leaving the room poorly illuminated. Chee-Chee and I had trouble seeing in the gloomy space.

When we told him why we were in his room, Cousin Charlie immediately began patting the pockets of his overalls, hunting his hidden cache.

"I know it's here somewhere," Cousin Charlie repeated a few times as he continued to hunt, groping in one pocket and then the next. We were not in any particular hurry, so waiting for Cousin Charlie to locate his money was not a problem, but for some reason Chee-Chee had a silly grin on her face. The goofy look puzzled me, but I said nothing. Finally, she could contain herself no longer. Chee-Chee glanced over at me with a sly look, one I had learned from vast experience not to trust.

With a glance toward Cousin Charlie she quipped, "You want me to turn the light on so you can see better."

I just about fell apart. Her words had been for my ears only, so although he did not hear what she said he knew she had spoken.

"Say what?" Cousin Charlie asked, still patting his pockets.

By now Chee-Chee and I were both laughing so hard, silently of course, that we could not have answered him even if we'd had a handy response. Our bodies shook violently as we struggled to contain the laughter threatening to bubble up and out of our mouths. "Nothing," one of us finally managed to mumble. Cousin Charlie was never the wiser.

It was a big, major *No! No!* to laugh at or make fun of the elders in any way. This simply was not done, and certainly not right in front of them. Our behinds would have been in a sling for sure if Auntie had heard us and reported to our parents. She did not, though, or I would not still be alive to tell about it.

No amount of light would have helped blind Cousin Charlie find his money. He would not have been able to see his hand in front of his face even if we had hung the sun from his ceiling.

Cousin Charlie finally found his money in the very last pocket he searched. He handed it over to us and we were on our way. Moments later, Chee-Chee and I were out the door, our chests still heaving with the effort of suppressing our giggles.

Soon Chee-Chee and I were far enough away from Auntie's house to safely express our mirth. The laughter that had been threatening to overflow began to spring forth. We snickered until our sides ached and the tears flowed freely down our cheeks. We carried on loudly, giving no thought to the fact that, since we were far enough away from Auntie's house to not have to worry about her hearing us laughing, we must necessarily be close enough to the church for those folks to hear us.

Sure enough, as soon as we got inside the sanctuary several people asked us what we had been laughing so hard about. We spared the adults (ourselves really) the truth, quickly concocting a creative lie about a lizard we mistook for a snake. They thought us exceptionally silly anyway, so it was easy to convince the older folks that we had been laughing innocently.

To our partners and siblings—Sister Girl, Big Sister and Jeffie Mae—we told the truth. They laughed heartily but without the insight that Chee-Chee and I had. We had been there!

I still laugh when I think of that incident.

CHAPTER 18: FAYE, BYRD, AND SISTER GIRL'S SKIRT

My siblings and I frequently enjoy ourselves at the expense of the other members of the family. There is no question: we "got it honest," and it started early. It seems that poor Sister Girl was often the recipient of someone's ire.

It seems like just yesterday that Faye and Byrd decided to "break her up from carrying tales." It did not matter to the pair that much of the information Sister Girl told was factual, the older girls simply did not appreciate being told on—not one bit. She was a vicious tattler and needed to be taught a lesson. Faye and Byrd were just plain sick and tired of Sister Girl. They couldn't wait for an opportunity to get her back for telling Mama something or other about them. Their chance came in a most unusual "fashion."

These were the days of poodle skirts, fishnet stockings, and cashmere sweaters. Tight, slinky skirts and Capri pants were also fashionable. Faye and Byrd were talented seamstresses and did well keeping themselves in near to the height of fashion, putting Mama's treadle-operated Singer sewing machine to good use. They worked wonders with the fifty-pound sacks that flour came in.

Everybody used these sacks to make clothes and household items, so there was no shame being seen in a "flour sack" dress. The prints on the cloth were really quite attractive: flowers, birds and other designs, as well as bright colors combined to make a decent presentation when formed into a garment. The truly talented (or the really desperate) could even make underwear from these sacks.

Byrd and Faye had made themselves several "straight" skirts using this material. The skirts were quite snug through the hips and thighs, with an elasticized waist. Sister Girl was notably impressed with her older sisters' talents. She wanted one of those skirts.

Fortunately for her, Faye and Byrd could be very kind and considerate on occasion. Unfortunately for her, they could also

Faye, in high school

wrap vindictiveness in a cloak of kindness to the point that the unsuspecting victim was taken completely unawares.

On this fateful Saturday morn Sister Girl was being particularly worrisome. She wanted a skirt, was determined to have one, and was never going to stop bugging Faye and Byrd until they produced one for her. They didn't want to do it because they were, as always, mad at Sister Girl for a recent infraction. Sister Girl was determined; she begged and begged, irritating the girls more and more. It finally reached the point that normally mild-mannered Faye Eddie told Sister Girl that she was "worrying the dog sh-- out of her."

Sister would not be stopped. Faye and Byrd were furious and so began to conspire between themselves regarding the fashioning of this skirt and how they could use it in a way to make Sister Girl sorry she had ever asked for it—not to mention sorry that she had ever told on them.

The older girls rummaged through the flour sack collection until they came up with one they thought suitable for their younger sister. They used Sister Girl's very ample body as their live model. They probably would have made Sister Girl a decent skirt and let their animosity die a natural death, but this child would not let well enough alone. She wanted the skirt made to her exact specifications, not hesitating one moment to issue one directive after another.

"I want this part tighter than this part," Sister Girl whined. On and on she went. "I don't like the way these flowers look . . . move this part over here."

Foolish nitwit!

Finally, Byrd and Faye had the skirt finished, as close to Sister Girl's demands as they could get. They were talented seamstresses but they were not miracle workers. A miracle is what Sister Girl needed, though she didn't know it at the time.

When the skirt was finished, it was so tight Sister Girl could hardly sit down. But she was happy. She twitched around the house all morning, her fat butt waddling all over the house.

She acted as if she were sporting an Oscar de la Renta original and had the figure for it. Do I need to tell you that this was not the case? I thought not. After all, I have already said that it was Faye and Byrd making the skirt; I never mentioned an Oscar (although they could have been awarded one for the performance they put on later that same day).

Sister Girl showed off her skirt to anyone who was unfortunate enough to be in her path. She thought she was really something. That, at least, was true: she was something. Indeed she was.

Toward the late afternoon the older girls decided to walk down to visit Uncle Floyd and Aunt Odessa. Naturally, Sister Girl wanted to tag along, anxious to show off her new skirt. (Some people have no sense of imminent doom before it strikes.) The older girls let Sister Girl go with them. Little did she know those devils had a trap set for her.

The trip to Uncle Floyd and Aunt 'Dessa's took a bit longer than the usual seven or eight minutes. Sister Girl had to walk carefully and slowly in honor of her new skirt being so tight. She begged Faye and Byrd to wait on her and they did, very patient and kind. Sister Girl should have been at least a little suspicious by now, but she wasn't. As I said, some people have no idea when disaster is about to pay a visitation upon them.

The girls enjoyed a pleasant visit with our aunt and uncle. As he often did, Uncle Floyd plied Sister Girl with a huge box of two dozen candy bars, admonishing her to share. She had no intention of doing so. Sister Girl was already busy planning an appropriate hiding place for the candy. It was the smug expression on her face that sealed her fate.

They prepared to leave. By now it had grown late in the evening; the sun had gone down, though there was still a hint of its orange glow in the far western sky.

After bidding Aunt Odessa and Uncle Floyd a fond farewell, the trio struck out for home. Byrd and Faye walked nice and slow so that Sister Girl could keep up with them—until they got out of sight of Floyd and Odessa. The girls then sprang their trap.

They quickly picked up the pace, leaving poor Sister Girl hard-pressed to keep up with them. Not only was her skirt too tight, but she was also holding that big box of butter fingers, a double handicap. Faye and Byrd began to run.

Uh oh! Sister Girl took off after them, her skirt beginning to split along the side seam. Byrd and Faye ran faster.

Sister Girl began crying after them, begging them to slow down.

It was dark by now, and she was afraid. In spite of all her big talk, Sister Girl was basically a coward, afraid of her own shadow.

Her skirt began to split on the other side. By now the tails of the skirt were flapping in the gusts of wind Sister Girl created every time her chubby thighs slapped together.

It was pitch black. Sister began to cry in earnest, still hanging onto the candy box, skirt flapping, the split climbing higher and higher up her thighs.

The miscreants ran so fast that they arrived home a full three minutes before Sister Girl came lumbering over the hill screaming and crying, claiming that the "haints" had tried to get her. She managed to hang onto the candy, though. By the time the poor girl made it into the house, her skirt was being held on her body by nothing but the elastic in the waistband, the seams on both sides completely undone.

Needless to say, Byrd and Faye were rolling with laughter. Their plan for revenge had worked even better than they had planned. They hadn't counted on the "candy factor." Once Uncle Floyd handed Sister Girl that box and she stupidly let it be known that she wasn't going to share it, her fate was effectively sealed. The older girls did not find out until later in the week that Aunt Odessa had witnessed more of the scene than they thought as she stood in her yard.

In fact, she had been able to see enough of the show to easily figure out what was going on. She didn't tell her husband, astutely guessing that he would have jumped in his old GMC and dashed to Sister Girl's rescue. Aunt 'Dessa, on the other hand, quite agreed with Faye and Byrd that although she was her and her husband's pick, Sister Girl did need to be taught a lesson—or two.

CHAPTER 19: THE BEAUTIFICATION OF THE YOUNG AND FOOLISH

Saturday mornings, or more often Friday evenings, heralded the beginning of the beautification ritual. First, there was the washing and the drying. No one in the community had a blow dryer in those days. In fact, I don't believe blow dryers for the home were widely available yet. If you can imagine such a time. Anyway, back in those days, it took all night or most of a day to air-dry one's hair.

Once the hair was clean and towel-dried, Mama or an older sister undertook the massive task of combing out the tangles. (Back then, tangles were called "naps," and not associated with needing sleep.) Naps were notoriously stubborn little buggers. They still are. Getting them out was accomplished amidst facial grimaces and occasional yelps. The tools chosen were of vital importance. The wider the spaces between the teeth of the comb, the easier it was to tug through the hair. I often wished someone would invent a comb with the teeth spaced as far apart as a yard rake. It never happened.

It did no good to complain to the comber about the pain, no matter how much it hurt. Such belly-aching only pissed off the person who was combing your hair, then she jerked that much harder. So, amidst admonishments to "hold still, turn this way, turn that way, be still," the deed was done.

When finished, our heads were adorned with at least a dozen small plaits. The smaller the plaits, the quicker the hair dried. Once the hair was dry the next stage began. Pressing! This is not quite the same as pressing clothes. Pressing hair was even more torturous. Clothes are devoid of feeling, therefore, the heat from a hot iron meant nothing to them. On the other hand, our heads certainly felt the heat from the straightening comb when our hair was being pressed. It meant plenty to us.

Uncle Floyd's wife, our Aunt Odessa, was the local beautician. I imagine she had graduated from some obscure cosmetology school many decades before. She did not bother to keep up with the latest styles and kept absolutely no chemicals in her home shop whatsoever. You came to her knowing exactly what the choices were—a press or a press and curl.

To begin, Aunt Odessa sat us down in one of her cane-bottomed, straight, ladder-backed chairs. No swiveling hydraulic lift stools for her. The single element hot plate she used was plugged in, and her instruments of torture were placed on it to heat. Aunt Odessa never owned one of those fancy "stations" that no modern beautician would be without. She used a blue wooden stand Uncle Floyd crafted for her to keep her implements handy.

The stand was about four and a half feet tall, so she did not have to bend or stoop to reach her tools. Her hot plate sat on top, and there was a shelf underneath where she stored her curling irons and straightening combs and, of course, the requisite white cotton rags. She also kept a spare jar of pressing oil there, usually Mus-Ro or Royal Crown. We were supposed to bring our own hair dressing, but if we forgot or did not have any, she used hers.

The hot combs and Marcel irons (hot curlers) were placed on the heating element for a few moments. Auntie then began the arduous process of unbraiding and sectioning the hair, usually beginning at the nape of the neck. After taking all the hair down, Aunt Odessa then nimbly ran her fingers throughout the entire mop, checking out its condition and dryness. Woe unto those whose hair was not completely dry.

If the hair was still damp Auntie dried it out by quickly dragging a hot comb through the moist strands. Steam rose from the head as Aunt Odessa dried the hair in this fashion. Sitting very still was paramount; if we moved we were surely burned. When that happened our bodies rose even higher than the steam. Nothing burned quite as badly as a steamed head.

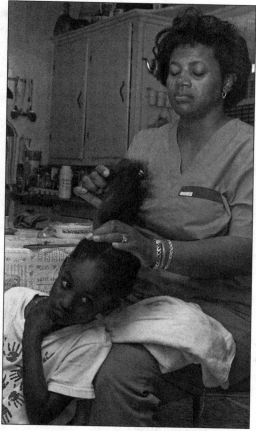

Beatrice works on Sherrell's hair

Once the hair was moisture-free, Aunt 'Dessa began the task of sectioning and pulling the locks. She used her left hand to separate small bunches of hair into even smaller clusters of less than a half inch in diameter. She used her forefinger for this task, hooking it under the bit of hair, separating it near the scalp from the rest while at the same time applying a dab of hair oil along the shaft. With her right hand she grasped the now smoking Marcel curling iron from the hot plate. (Auntie's homemade work stand was just past waist high, so she did not have to sit to do her work, preferring, as she did, to stand behind her patrons.)

Hot curling iron firmly in hand, Aunt 'Dessa began "pulling" the hair. She deftly opened and snapped the irons shut, rolling and clicking the handles all the while. All this clicking and rolling served to move air through the irons, effectively cooling them. Pulling the hair, technically, is not the same as pressing. Pulling referred to the process outlined above. That is, using Marcel irons to straighten the hair. Pressing, on the other hand, involved the use of hot combs to straighten the hair.

The hot irons warmed the neck as Auntie brought the implement toward the hair roots. She made contact with the hair no more than 1/8 of an inch away from the scalp. How she got so close I will never know. I was mildly burned only once or twice during the ten years Auntie did my hair, quite a testament to her skill.

The hot curling iron was rapidly pulled through the hair, leaving straightness in its wake. The pulling was accompanied by the unmistakable sizzle of hot oil melting on the hair shaft. It was an interesting sound, a soft hiss combined with the "click-clack" of the ceramic handles as they rolled around the steel rods which gave them substance. This process was repeated time and again, section by section, until the whole head was done.

Finally, the hair was slick and glossy and as straight as it could possibly be. What began as short nappy plaits was now a long rectilinear mane.

If the hair was to be straightened only and not also curled, the process was complete. Aunt 'Dessa drew the entire shank of hair, if you had enough, into a pony tail and secured it with a rubber band. If she were feeling really creative she curled your bangs using the same Marcel irons that she had just pulled your brains out with.

Having our hair pulled was not terribly painful. In fact, I found it so relaxing that I occasionally dozed off. Aunt Odessa did not permit that and quickly admonished me. "Ain't no sleeping on this train," she said. I woke up immediately and stayed awake for the rest of the session. Although it never happened, I was always afraid that if I dared to doze again Auntie's next statement on the subject would be, "Oops, sorry."

Aunt Odessa was so good at her profession that women came from miles around, and paid their fifty cents (a dollar for pulling and curling) to get their hair done. Auntie only did straightening or pulling and curling. She did not do permanents or even roller sets, nor did she offer shampoo service. She did not do dye jobs, tints, weaves, bonding, braiding, or anything like that. Oh, and she did not do men.

Straightening or pulling and curling, that was it. It! Haircutting and styling were not offered, either. The only time she ever picked up a pair of scissors was after she accidentally scorched a bit of hair. That happened rarely.

Patrons could not call and make appointments for my aunt's services. In the early days before 1967, no one in our community had a telephone, and anyway, Auntie only did hair on Saturday. In case of emergency, such as a death in the family or on special occasions such as graduations, Aunt Odessa would fix hair. Generally, though, if someone's hair needed beautifying, she simply showed up on Saturday and waited her turn.

During the summer wise patrons arrived before 9:00 AM. Waiting until the day grew hot meant running the risk that the hairdo would immediately fail as soon as it was exposed to the ubiquitous humidity.

Aunt Odessa was the main source of straight hair back in those days, but most women and older girls could fire up their own and each other's heads if the need arose. Usually, this was done in the kitchen, where there was often a fire smoldering in the huge wood-burning stove.

Mama began her beautifying process in this manner. First, she opened the fire door to the stove (this is the chamber where the wood was actually burned) and placed an empty vegetable can in the red-hot coals, half-burying it in the glowing embers. She put the straightening comb in the can, being careful to keep the wooden handle away from the hot coals. It took about a minute for the comb to heat up the first time; after that initial firing the comb was usually ready in about thirty seconds. When Mama withdrew the comb it was smoking, hot and ready to straighten hair.

To test the heat of the comb and to clean off any excess grease or accidentally accumulated ashes, Mama swiftly rubbed the hot comb across a folded white cotton rag handily draped over her knees. If the comb did not scorch the cloth too badly Mama grabbed a hunk of hair (about an inch in diameter) and slowly dragged the comb through it. Straightening the hair with hot combs instead of pulling it with Marcel irons left it fluffier and a bit less straight. The advantage was that it took consider-ably less time.

Mama always hot-combed our hair to straighten it. She never pulled it. I don't think she knew how. I certainly did not want her to learn on my hair. Instead, she used heavy, metal-toothed combs made for one purpose: straightening hair. The handle on one of her combs originally had a wood casing over the steel insert. The wood part burned away as a result of the comb resting too far inside the fire chamber. This particular comb had wickedly curved steel teeth.

I hated that comb. The bare metal handle grew very hot when placed in the stove. I had experienced the effects of personal contact with its hot metal handle and was wary of it. Mama owned an array of hot combs, but for some dubious reason she preferred that one. (We did know what a "sadist" was back then. Well, we knew what one was, we were just ignorant of the terminology.)

Mama always wrapped the handles of whichever comb she was using in a wad of cloth before pulling it out of the can. Sometimes, though, the cloth was not substantial enough and the heat would pass through to Mama's hand. When that happened we would do well to have anticipated it by the way Mama tried to juggle the comb.

If you knew what was going on you quickly slid out of the way. If we did not catch on soon enough or weren't fast enough to get out of the way, we were in for a very bad time. When the comb became too hot for Mama to handle, altruistic though she was, she was not likely to drop it on her own legs.

To her credit Mama always tried to keep the hot comb from slithering down our backs, but sometimes she wasn't quick enough and the worst happened. If you did not move when she did let go of the comb, the only place it could go was on her legs or down your back. Down one's back it went if the unlucky lady was inexperienced or mentally deranged enough to still be sitting there between Mama's legs.

If you were wise and fast, the comb simply slid to the floor, perhaps scorching the linoleum, but no matter about that.

Mama was pretty good with a straightening comb, but she did not have Aunt Odessa's skill and finesse. We sat with fear and trembled between our mother's legs, the hard kitchen floor beneath us adding to our discomfiture. Some of our lengthiest and most earnest praying was done in that position. We often beseeched God to help Mama keep the hot comb from singeing our necks, backs, and ears. Many times we were blessed, our prayers answered. Alas, there were occasions when we girls had to contend with the unmistakable print from a hot comb on the back of our neck.

The abhorrent curved-tooth comb left a particularly interesting burn print, different from its straight-toothed counterparts.

No matter the design, straight or curved, it hurt to have a hot comb scorch tender bare skin. The marks were visible for weeks, weeks that seemed like years as we explained to curious folks what had caused the stripes on our necks.

The curious were almost always male. Males without sisters, I might add. Certainly every black female in America, young or old, easily recognized hot comb prints and could do so from about a mile away.

Peers dared not laugh. All the other girls knew what it was like to be so injured. Straightening hair with heat was a very common practice then and now. There is not a female alive or dead who had her hair straightened or pulled without getting burned.

When Mama finished straightening our hair she "bumped" our bangs. This process involved folding a section of hair around the teeth of the comb. The hair was then dragged through the comb with a bumping motion. The result was a looser curl than Marcel irons imparted.

While the hair was still hot we hurriedly rolled it in sponge rollers. If none were available, we used a torn strip of paper bag which had been folded into strips about one-half inch wide. The section of hair was wound around the paper, then the ends of the paper were tied in a simple knot. Rolling hair on these paper strips was a true art form. Even more artful was the way we looked with twisted lengths of tied paper bag strips dotting our heads.

After all that torture in the name of beauty, it is no wonder we felt we had to somehow adorn our hair. We suffered mightily for that hair; surely the surveyors would never begrudge a bunch of tortured, nappy-headed, ribbon-less girls a few plastic guide ribbons.

I think not. In fact, I am certain they would have been impressed with our creativity had they the opportunity to witness it. Of course, they never did. We never let them know what happened to their ribbons.

CHAPTER 20: TOYS, PLAY-PRETTIES, AND OTHER AMUSEMENTS

Growing up in rural surroundings encouraged us children to use our imaginations in many areas. Not only were we creative in the use of those tacky plastic ribbons, but we enterprisingly used other readily available items as well. We were most ingenious in the fabrications of toys, games, and play-pretties. One of our most popular creations was the "sand roller."

Back in the olden days (pre-1970), Clabber Girl baking powder came in a heavy aluminum can with a fitted lid made of the same material. These days Clabber Girl comes in aluminum-lined paper containers which are closed with a plastic-seal lid. They just don't make anything like they used to. I remember when we could pour used, hot cooking grease back into an empty Crisco can. No one does that anymore because the "cans" are made of aluminum-lined paper, just like modern-day baking powder containers.

When the baking powder was all used up Mama gave us kids the empty can to use for sand rollers. We could count on getting a can about once a month. These were the days when biscuits came from the kitchen and not from the dough boy. Even the largest can of baking powder did not last long.

We took our treasure outside, filled it with about three cups of the sandy, cinnamon-colored dirt common to our region. A few small rocks added a gentle "clink-clink" to the otherwise mushy sound effects of the sand roller in action.

After the can was filled, holes were punched in the top and bottom with a hammer or sturdy object (a shoe, piece of wood, or some unsuspecting youngster's head) and a medium-sized nail. We then threaded a long piece of wire through the holes and tied it off about three inches from the base of the sand roller. Two coat hangers, unwrapped and tied together to make one long wire, worked quite nicely for this, and coat hangers were easy to come by. Occasionally, we lucked upon a piece of hay-baling wire, nicer material than coat hangers because it was long enough to not require splicing.

After the wire was strung through the can we fashioned a handle out of the tail-end, making sure it was large enough to slip our fingers through for a good grip. The only thing left to do after that was to take the roller for a spin.

The toy worked perfectly if it rolled smoothly and evenly with just a little stream of dirt seeping through the nail holes. If the holes were too big, too much dirt fell through, necessitating frequent refills. If the holes were too small, the roller would simply not turn at all and the roller dragged instead of rolling.

We took the newly crafted toy up the road a piece then back down again, taking in the sights as we trotted along, sand roller gliding smoothly behind us. We raced each other with fierce competition, often constructing obstacle courses to make the event more challenging.

Whether racing or leisurely trolling the roller, it was always imperative to keep it on a straight course, never allowing it to tilt. We did not have to worry much about distractions along the roadway. There was nothing to see that we had not seen a million times before. Trees, bushes, berry vines, an occasional rabbit or squirrel, that's about all. But we prudently kept our ears open for the sound of approaching vehicles.

Sometimes, we concentrated so intently on watching our rollers that we failed to navigate around the biggest obstacles of all—each other. More than a few times, two or more of us kids collided with a bang, sounding amazingly like big horn sheep engaged in head butting. Such collisions are possibly the source of at least some of our questionable cognitive abilities, and were a readily accepted part of growing up in some of the most serene territory in the nation.

After we tired of playing with sand rollers we moved on to other self-made amusements. My father seemed to always have a bunch of old tires around the property. In those days many people called them "caissons" (or maybe the spelling is "casein," I'm not sure). In any case, this is how you spell what we used the tires for: a-u-t-o-m-o-b-i-l-e. I do not mean to say that we kids used the tires *for* our automobiles, I mean we used the tires *as* our automobiles.

"How," you may well ask, "can one tire possibly substitute for a whole car?" Well, a bit of imagination and a tad of desperation for something to ease boredom made this magical transformation possible.

Each of us would grab a tire. Tires come in all sizes, so it was important to get one that fit the driver. There was an occasion when one of us (name withheld to protect the stupid one and his parents) tried to roll a tractor tire. Needless to say, the tire soon gained the upper hand, ultimately rolling the driver instead of the other way around. He was lucky to escape with his life and no more than a badly sprained ankle.

Once the tires were chosen, we pushed them slowly up the hill to the corner, a distance of about fifty yards. When we got to the corner, we queued up horizontally. While waiting for the starting "shot" we rocked our cars back and forth, making appropriate car-like noises all the while as we readied them for the race. An honorable designee would sound the count. "On your mark. Get set . . . Go!" (That was the count we used until our pa Butch taught us this one: "One for the money. Two for the show. Three to get ready. Four to go!") We liked the new one better, even though we had no idea that such terminology was connected with horse racing and, accordingly, gambling.

At the sound of "go" we dashed off. Because our race-track was down-hill, one or two good pushes was all the tires needed to become mobile. After that the true test of skill was keeping up with the tire and keeping it on course. The first person down the hill was not necessarily the winner. The winner was the first person who arrived down the hill with his tire. Many times the tire got away from the driver, sometimes rolling all the way to the branch in the road at the bottom of the hill, its driver racing frantically to catch it.

Tires were not the only things we rolled down hills. My brothers Pete and Tenchie, probably a few others as well, tried their hands at rolling fifty-five gallon steel barrels. There was real danger in rolling the unwieldy barrels. One of those boys broke his leg trying to foolishly roll a barrel while standing fully upright. He did not stand on it very long. After one or two turns the barrel flipped him onto the ground and ran right over him. I did not see this, but I heard about it.

CHAPTER 21: JOKES, TALES, AND OTHER LIES

The folks I grew up around were notorious tale tellers, anything to get a laugh. Here are a few samples.

My mother told this one:

> One time a man was walking home late at night. He decided to take a shortcut through the cemetery. As he walked along he found himself suddenly falling into a freshly opened grave.
>
> It was very cold that night and soon the man, clad only in a thin overcoat, began to shiver. He moaned and groaned, "Oh, it's so cold down here." He'd repeat himself every few minutes. "Oh, it's so cold down here."
>
> By and by another fellow happened along. This gent had spent the evening drinking at a local tavern. He was quite inebriated. To help hurry himself along home he, too, decided upon a shortcut, the same one through the cemetery that the first man had taken.
>
> As he passed near the open grave the second man heard the first gentleman. "Oh, it's so cold down here."
>
> The drunk walked over to the grave, much more curious than afraid.
>
> "No wonder you're cold!" he exclaimed. "You done kicked all the cover off you."

This one was Uncle N. E.'s favorite:

> One time the devil was out engaging in his usual Saturday night activity, going around to all the juke joints and honky tonks, gathering up sinners.
>
> He had sinners in both arms and sinners in his mouth. There were sinners everywhere; he had so many he could hardly hold them all.
>
> Well, it just so happened that as he started back toward Hell with his passel of sinners, he met a man who was on his

way to the store. This man knew the devil and what he was about.

"I see you got a bunch of 'em tonight, huh, devil?"

The devil, proud of his catch, replied, "Yep! I sure do."

You can deduce what happened. When he opened his mouth to speak, the sinners he had been carrying gripped between his teeth fell out and escaped. As they began to drop to the ground the devil started trying to grab them up. Oops! There went the ones he had been holding in his arms. The whole bunch escaped. Now this pissed off the devil mightily.

The next Saturday night the devil redoubled his efforts, finding twice as many sinners as he had the week before.

As he started back toward Hell he met the same man again.

"Got a real big bunch this week, huh, devil?" The devil had learned his lesson. He looked back at the man as he continued on toward Hell, grunting as he passed. "Uh-huh."

Speaking of Hell, Maye tells one on a similar subject:

There was an old man who went to the graveside services of a friend. The presiding undertaker took one look at the decrepit old man and said. "Ain't no use in you going home, you may as well stay since you're already here."

The Master Storyteller—my brother-in-law, Richard—tells stories that are our version of *Poor Richard's Almanack*. He swears these stories are true. I'll let you decide:

Richard says that when he was a boy (a long time ago), his family owned an old cow with the bad habit of getting into other people's crops. Richard says his daddy soon got tired of having to go catch the cow and drag her kicking and screaming out of folks' peas.

One day Pa sneaked up behind the cow as she snacked on purple hulls, with a jar of Hi-Lite in his hand. [Hi-Lite is a very potent acid-based product; people used to use it to discourage animals from coming around. The stuff literally burned the hide off anything it touched.]

Pa tossed about a cup of the vile liquid onto the cow's backside. The cow continued grazing, unaware that momentous events were occurring. Soon, the chemical began to do its work, burning through the hair on the cow's back.

The cow suddenly stopped chewing, raising her head in alarm, a puzzled expression on her face.

Richard says the cow whipped herself around, threw first one leg over her shoulder and then the other, frantically pawing her back as she hurried on her two back legs. The cow quickly reached the nearby creek, pawing her back with her front legs, prancing along with her hind legs. To the water she ran, jumped in, and promptly drowned.

Another one of Richard's:

One day Richard and his cousin were riding along in Richard's pickup truck. It was a warm, sunny summer day, so both windows were fully rolled down as the pair drove to their favorite fishing hole.

A few miles from the creek they came upon a snake, long and black. Richard pressed the gas pedal, speeding up so he could run over the big snake.

When the truck wheels made contact with the snake his tail came up and slapped inside the truck through the open window. Richard claims that while the snake's tail was wiggling on one side, his head was snapping at him through the other window.

They hurried on, finally dislodging the snake.

That story so impressed my family that, after we heard it, we changed our method of dealing with snakes. When we see a snake crossing the road, before we speed up the car to run over it, we first roll up all the windows. We practice this without fail, giving all the credit to Richard.

Sometimes jokes aren't told. They happen:

> One Sunday afternoon Maye, Sister Girl, Bubba, Gus, Mama, Butch, and I were sitting out on the front porch, engaged in a lengthy discussion about how it came to be that all us kids called our father (Butch) "Missonnell."
>
> He wasn't gay or anything. Mama had three children from a previous marriage. When she and Missonnell got together these kids were very young. I suppose Missonnell was a name her firstborn, E. J., came up with because he didn't want anybody calling him "daddy." The older kids called him Mister Monell, or rather, they tried to call him that. With each new child the term became more and more adulterated, ending up sounding like "Missonnell."
>
> As we sat talking and laughing about this Maye smarted off, singing this off-take of the song "Soon I Will be Done with the Troubles of the World": "Missonnell will be done with the troubles of the world, the troubles of the world, troubles of the world. Missonnell will be done with the troubles of the world. . . ."
>
> If you aren't familiar with the late gospel great Mahalia Jackson and the song she made famous in the movie *Imitation of Life*, this will make absolutely no sense to you. Go rent the movie. It's a classic.

Monel Upshaw, aka Missonnell, or Butch

We laughed quietly but without much heart. Missonnell was eighty-six at the time. While he had been blessed with unusually good health most of his life, his love of pork had led to a stroke the year before. This song was a bit too close for comfort, so although we appreciated Maye's wit, we just couldn't get into it too much.

CHAPTER 22:
DR. MAYE AND THE
INNOCENT FROG

Maye could always be counted on to provide a laugh or two. I remember the time Byrd had my whole body fairly shaking with mirth in the choir loft. We were at church one Sunday, and Maye was playing the piano for the choir, as usual.

What was unusual about that particular Sunday was that, unbeknownst to Maye, Byrd and I were planning a semi-surprise appreciation service for her hard work. (It is hard work banging a piano for a bunch of "no talents.") We were trying to decide whether we should "roast" Maye or just have a plain old church service. I leaned heavily toward roasting myself, but I don't believe Byrd had the nerve to go along with it.

After the choir finished bellowing out "All My Help Comes from the Lord," Byrd and I ducked our heads in conference. Byrd said she ought to tell at the appreciation service the story of her and Maye operating on a frog.

"Operating on a frog?" I asked in only mild astonishment. I knew these to be (Byrd and Maye) part of the trio (Faye was the third) who washed the cat in our old Maytag wringer washing machine, so I can't pretend that I was too surprised at anything they did. I was very interested in hearing the story of this surgical procedure, encouraging her to give me the details right then and there. We ducked our heads lower.

"A long time ago," Byrd began, "Maye and I caught a frog in the front yard. It was Maye's idea to open him up and see what his insides looked like." Byrd was really getting into her story by now and I was already shaking with gales of silent laughter.

Byrd continued, regaling me with the details of the dastardly deed. "We got one of Butch's new double-edged Gillette razors." Byrd chuckled as she went on with the story. "I held the frog flat on his back with his legs stretched out (being careful not to let him pee on my fingers, because that would have caused warts) and Maye sliced him open with the razor." Byrd added that Maye did the job very meticulously. "When she finished the frog had a very straight, neat incision that looked like an 'H' lying on its side. His whole belly was splayed open." Byrd says that in her hurry to begin the surgery she had forgotten to bring out anything to sew the frog back up with.

"I ran into the house [the surgical arena was the front porch] and fetched a spool of white quilting thread and a small sewing needle. Maye was poking around in the frog's guts, moving things from side to side with a pair of Missonnell's tweezers." Fearing for the frog, Byrd begged Maye to stop poking at him. "I resumed my post as chief assistant while Maye began to finally sew the frog back up."

I needed clarification. "You mean she actually sewed the incision back together?"

"Yep," Byrd went on. "She whipped him back up."

By this time I was laughing so hard I was sure the congregation thought I was having a profound religious experience. We ducked our heads lower still, now hiding behind hymnals in an attempt to hide our convulsions.

I had to know. "What happened to the frog? Did he die?"

Byrd stopped giggling long enough to answer. "We let him go and he hopped on off under the porch, but you know he went on and died."

"Maybe he didn't."

Byrd looked over at me like I was the one who was crazy. "You know he did."

"Byrd," I said, just wondering aloud, "how old were y'all when you did this?"

"I was just a kid," she replied, "but Maye was a big ole 'stand-up-in-the-road.'"

That did it, I just flat-out howled. It's a good thing for the pair of us that our brother-in-law Hadie (the surgeon's husband) was

Hadie Hamm praying

praying at the time. Byrd and I needn't have feared that anyone would hear us laughing in the choir loft . . . when Hadie prays nothing else stands a chance.

I suggested to Byrd that she should tell that story during the appreciation service. I'm sure the congregation would have been quite amused to learn that the esteemed Mrs. Ham actually began her quest for knowledge long before she reached college.

The services were held a few weeks later. Byrd refused to tell the story, so I felt it my Christian duty to enlighten the folks about who it was they were "appreciating."

Maye was as surprised as the congregation was when I started telling the tale; she had no idea I even knew about the frog story. She sat there stupefied as I repeated what Byrd had told me, embellishing only a bit.

Maye was feeling pretty full of herself, appreciated and all, so she didn't mind about my telling the story. She thoroughly enjoyed herself that day except for one tense moment, and it wasn't the moment I started telling the frog story. I will elucidate.

Beatrice, 1976

I sometimes feel quite creative. I was born under the sign of Taurus and, according to astrological lore, I am supposed to be talented with a wonderful singing voice, creative in an artistic fashion, and an all-around wonderful influence (that to make up for my stubbornness).

The truth is, no matter what the stars say, I cannot sing, I cannot paint, draw, or sculpt, I cannot weave, mold or spin—I will let you decide if I can even write. Sporadically, though, I feel the need to undertake some artistic endeavor just to remind myself that the stars were mistaken. On the occasion of the appreciation I decided to make (create) a corsage for Maye to wear on her shoulder. I called her and inquired about the physical characteristics of the clothing she'd be wearing. It didn't really matter what she'd planned; she would have to conform to my color scheme.

I strongly suggested that she wear something aesthetically compatible with the colors wine and hunter green. Maye had something else in mind, implying that her new red dress was quite becoming.

Red doesn't go with wine. I know Maye wanted to look nice for the occasion, and I suppose it was rather foolish of me to wait until after I had made the corsage before I asked what her color scheme was.

I had wandered through the silk flower aisles at Wal-Mart for more than two hours, trying to come up with a vision of something extraordinary. I gave up on extraordinary and settled for fairly presentable. I'd paid for my purchases and hurried home to begin ministering to the flowers and other baubles I had bought. What I came up with actually looked quite nice. Maye would just have to fall in line.

After I finished my creation I put it in a plain white florist's box. The next day—Sunday, right before Maye was escorted into the sanctuary from her hideout in the cafeteria—I asked her daughter Teri to grace her body with the corsage. They both exclaimed in wonder at its beauty. What a proud moment for me.

The service was soon underway and I forgot about the corsage and concentrated on "making out like" I was concentrating on the sermon. The minister spoke eloquently about . . . well, I don't remember the subject, but I do know it was appropriate and very well done. Suddenly, Maye jumped up—"jumped" is far too graphic and in such a negative sense. Rather, I should say she "rose" from her seat, caught my eye, and beckoned for me to follow her as she headed from the sanctuary to the cafeteria. I, too, "rose" from my seat and struck out in behind her.

I wondered briefly what could be wrong. Maye was walking in a most unusual posture with her head tilted to the left and with a most distinct list. Maye has a history of back trouble. *No doubt it's just rheumatism making her old back ache*, I thought to myself. After all, she was sitting on the front pew, and she had on kind of a tight skirt. I figured that trying to sit up straight while keeping her skirt down around her knees had placed undue stress on her vertebral alignment. This was what I surmised. Boy was I surprised.

When we got to the cafeteria, Maye about bowled me over with this testimony to my talent. She said that while she was sitting there concentrating on the sermon (just as I was, I'm sure), a bee had flown from somewhere toward the back of the sanctuary and landed smack dab in the middle of her corsage. Furthermore, the bee seemed quite content in the newly discovered oasis of silk posies and would not come out. Now this is rich!

"A bee?" I asked.

"Yes," Maye explained, "I was just sitting there and the lady on the pew behind me leaned forward and told me that a bee just flew into my flowers."

To my credit I did not laugh—not then, anyway. Maye said the reason she was walking with her head tilted was so as not to stir the bee up. We managed to get the bee out and killed without any tragedies—well, the bee might not agree. Later in the day Hadie, Maye's husband, laughingly remarked, "That bee was trying to get my honey."

CHAPTER 23:
JAMES BROWN

When the rest of the gang and I get together, it is understood that we must contrive to have, most of it, harmless fun. There are those of us, namely Bubba, Tenchie and Pete, who fancy themselves to have a talent for preaching. I don't mean "preaching" like you go to church to hear, I mean "preaching" like you would go to a comedy club to hear.

Their sermons generally reflect the type of upbringing we all shared, for they invariably bespeak of the "fire and brimstone" we lived in fear of when we were children. On this particular occasion—homecoming 1991—the brothers did their preaching on Saturday, leaving Sunday afternoon for them to play the devil. Brother Gene was in on this act, and he deserves an Academy Award for his portrayal of James Brown doing his signature tune "Please, Please, Please." It happened like this.

We were sitting under the gigantic oak tree, the arena for our outdoor activities whenever the weather permitted. A few years ago Pete laid a very nice concrete slab under the tree; it was large enough to easily hold outdoor furniture and other odds and ends. Pete had designed it so that the base of his barbecue pit was enclosed in concrete at the southeast corner of the slab. This way, while he worked his magic at the pit, we could provide him with entertainment and general conversation. Under the tree is where we were when Gene decided do his James Brown act, the idea occurring to him as he listened to Bobby Blue Bland's greatest hits. The next thing we knew Gene was sliding around on the concrete slab, imitating the famous "JB shuffle." This by itself was absolutely hilarious. If you've ever seen J. B. do his thing, you know exactly what I mean.

Gene crooned, "Please, please, please, don't go." On and on he went. It was wonderful; James himself would have been impressed. This wasn't good enough for Gene, though. It wasn't enough for him that we were falling out of our outdoor furniture practically rolling in the dirt with laughter. No! He wanted more. What did he do? He stopped! He exclaimed, "I need a cape." Think back to those old James Brown moves and you'll understand why the almighty cape was so important.

"A cape?" I can practically see Byrd's noodles whining as she wondered where to find a cape. It occurred to Byrd that Sister Girl had worn a black, circle-tailed skirt to church that very morning. Sister Girl had put the skirt in her car after church was over.

Byrd traipsed over to Sister Girl's Taurus and opened the door to the back. There, hanging on the hanger knob, was the skirt. "This would make a perfect cape for James," old "noodle head" surmised as she took the skirt over to Gene. He had all the props he needed after having picked up a stick to emulate a microphone. Byrd handed the skirt to Pete who was standing in for Fred, J. B.'s erstwhile band leader. Pete lost no time draping the skirt over Gene's shoulders as he kneeled on the pavement crooning. "Please, please, please, don't go, please . . . please, please, don't go. Oh, don't go, I love you so." Gene looked as pitiful and sincere as James ever did. His forehead even shone. The only thing lacking was a "process" on his hair.

Gene sang and moaned on. Then, true to James' style, he jumped up and threw Sister Girl's brand new—only been on her hide one time—skirt in the dust. Sister Girl was not under the tree when this scene occurred, but as luck would have it, she heard all the raucous laughter from inside the house and decided to come investigate. She arrived just in time to see her new skirt hit the dust.

Sister Girl quickly took in the scene. She had a fair idea of how this all had come to pass. Byrd was laughing the hardest, so Sister Girl figured that she was the party who'd taken the skirt from the car. Sister Girl was not too happy about her skirt standing in for James' cloak, but she had to admire the skill with which Gene executed James' moves. No matter—this was her brand new skirt.

Sister Girl hurried quickly to the "stage," not hesitating a moment as she snatched her skirt from the dust, fully intending to shake it out and put it back in her car, locking it this time. She must have sensed that they weren't through. "Please, please, please," Gene began again. "Hand me my cloak, Fred," he interjected. All eyes were on Sister Girl. *Was she going to spoil the fun?* was the silent question on everyone's minds. No one would have thought badly of her if she had gone ahead with her plan to lock her skirt safely in the trunk. She just would have been the subject of the next skit.

Sister Girl must have developed the ability to suddenly read minds, because she went ahead and draped the skirt back across Gene's dejected looking shoulders. "Don't go, oh, don't go, I love you so." We all thought Gene would give it up after this, but nooo! He jumped up and threw the girl's skirt in the dust a second time. This was too much. We never thought he would have this much nerve.

What did Sister do this time? She had a sick grin on her face, but she graciously picked up her skirt, unlocked her trunk and threw it in. Then she turned and walked back into the house without a backward glance. Pete and Gene howled with laughter. This one would go down in the history books. Well, here it is.

To her credit, Sister still acts "good graciously" when the story is told. This is just the way we behave when we get together.

CHAPTER 24: WASH DAY

I remember wash day as the day of the week we dreaded most. My sisters and I had the unenviable job of doing the laundry for the family. This was before the days of automatic washing machines—not that they had not been invented yet, just that no one in our community had one. No one in the entire community even knew how to operate a dryer much less owned one of those contraptions. To us, a dryer consisted of the three galvanized steel wire lines strung about three feet apart between two eight-foot-tall "T" poles on the south side of the house. The other components of the "dryer" were the wooden spring-type clothes pins used to affix the wet items to the line. We used a huge oval-shaped aluminum tub to haul the laundry to and from the clothes line in back of the house. All it took to complete the drying was the sun, a light breeze, and our nimble fingers to hang the wet pieces on the line.

Nowadays there are lots of television commercials depicting fluffy towels, and soft cotton sheets abound as something to be truly proud of. I suppose that could be a source of pride. There is certainly nothing wrong with clean laundry. What you don't see in the commercials is all the work it took to get them to that stage. Today it's hardly work at all—you just throw the dirty clothes into the washer, add some pollutants, and less than a half hour later the laundry is done. Back in those fabulous "olden" days, though, there was a bit more to it.

Wash day meant first building a hot fire under the old black iron pot. This pot was huge. I guess it held about, oh, thirty gallons of water or so. It felt more like twenty thousand when we were filling it up. Anyway, we'd build a hot fire and start the pot to boiling, finally dumping the dirty clothes in.

Every now and then we'd use Tide, but lye soap was plentiful, and cheaply made at home. For boiling really dirty clothes, lye soap worked better than commercial preparations anyway. This soap was made in the fall of the year, coinciding with hog-killing time. This made sense, as the soap was made from rendered pork fat, lye and ashes, and a few other ingredients. The soap was mixed up and cooked in the same pot we used for boiling clothes. After the soap had cooked for a while, it was ladled out of the pot and allowed to harden. Once it was firm enough, the soap was cut into the nice, fat pieces we used to boil clothes with.

In the real, real, olden days, lye was also used to clean bodies—live ones, I mean. This mixture was quite corrosive (to say the least), but it certainly was effective on tough greasy dirt. Perhaps I should make a commercial.

The clothes would boil for about 30–45 minutes or so, depending on how dirty they were. The dirtier they were the longer they "cooked." Every so often one of us would punch down the clothes in the pot, using a heavy wooden dowel to move the dirty laundry around in the bubbling pot.

After their time in the pot, the clothes were lifted from the boiling water with the same wooden pole, a few pieces at a time. The pole had to be wooden because metal would have quickly transferred the heat from the cooked clothing along the pole to your hands, then you would have dropped the pole and the clothes along with it. You not only would have been in trouble, but you would have had to do that boiling all over again.

After the clothes were retrieved from the pot they were transferred a few feet and were then dropped into a double-handled metal tub. We'd carry the tub the short distance to the shed which housed the washing machine. Sometimes the tub was so heavy my sister and I would slip a pole (metal was better for this task) through the handles of the tub and carry it suspended between us. This didn't happen too often, because I always caught Sister Girl trying to slide the tub more toward my end of the pole, giving me much of the weight to bear. She explained this discrepancy, claiming that because she was taller than I, the tub slid toward me due to gravitational force. Hmm.

Once we got to the shed, the wet clothes were dropped into the Maytag where they sloshed and rocked back and forth in the washer. I remember the outside of the washer was white porcelain-covered metal and the agitator was red, as were the rollers in the wringer (maybe the rollers were black, maybe they were beige; I don't really remember, but I do know the agitator was red).

After the clothes agitated a few minutes we'd begin the task of threading the clothing through the wringer. These were the two rollers which together squeezed the water from the clothing. The rollers were operated electrically and were therefore quite dangerous. On more than a few occasions one of us kids would get our fingers caught in the rollers. This caused a painful crushing sensation.

The sensor on the wringer was supposed to detect the difference between laundry and arms; if it did, the rollers would pop apart and you could then slide your arm out from between the rollers. If the sensor failed, a backup system allowed you to manually pop the rollers apart, that is, if you or someone could reach the lever at the top of the wringer to release the rollers. There was also a reverse switch that allowed you to "back" your appendage out of the rollers. The rollers would still be moving, of course, still mashing your limb, but at least you'd be moving out of the situation. If you were especially careless you could get your clothing—or worse, your hair—caught up in the rollers. The hair thing happened to Faye one time. What a way to "roll" your hair. Luckily, Byrd was close by and fairly quickly managed to release the rollers before Faye lost too much of her glory.

We got our hands, arms, and clothing caught in the wringer so often that, over time, the mechanism holding the two rollers together became so weakened that the rollers would automatically pop open if anything much thicker than a sock was introduced to it. When the wringer system became that ineffective, we'd dismantle the assembly and haul it off to the shop to be tightened up. After the repair, we knew to be very careful once again.

Some things could not be wrung out with the machine. Large items like bedspreads had to be wrung out by hand. Two of us would stretch the spread out between us, each grabbing an end. We'd twist and twist, making the spread or blanket shorter with each turn as the water was wrung out. This technique was rough on the arms and hands. I would swear that wringing out heavy laundry caused my carpal tunnel syndrome . . . if I suffered from it. Since I have no such affliction, I'll not lay the blame.

That old Maytag was used for a lot more than washing clothes. I mention elsewhere that Faye and Byrd once (or twice) used the washer to wash the cats, which was a mean thing to do—everyone knows that cats do not like water. This is, of course, why they did it.

The cats squalled and scratched, trying desperately to climb out of the machine. Byrd and Faye rolled with laughter. I don't suppose this little water play really hurt the cats. As far as I know, the two never passed the cats through the wringer.

In addition to posing as a pet washer, the appliance also stood in as a car from time to time. This was a "boy activity." Tenchie and Pete used to "drive" the machine whenever it was parked on the front porch instead of in the wash shed. The machine was on the porch before or after it had made a trip to the shop. Anyway, the boys would get behind the machine and push it around the perimeter of the porch, making car noises as they drove. Driving the machine was easy enough since the machine had four wheels, its only detectable similarity to an automobile.

One time, after the washer returned from the shop, the boys, in their enthusiasm and love for the "open road" of the porch, so vigorously drove their vehicle that it tipped off into the yard. There the Maytag lay on its side in my Mama's flower border.

Sister Girl and I never approved of the boys trying to make the machine into a car, but we always stuck together, protecting each other as needed. It was only right for us to try to help our brothers get the machine back up on the porch.

The boys pushed from the ground while Sister Girl and I pulled from the edge of the porch. We struggled and struggled to no avail. We pushed and pulled, then switched places. They pulled while we pushed. Nothing worked.

We did not know enough about engineering or the laws of physics or whatever it was that we needed to know to figure out how to get the machine back up on the porch. The distance from the porch to the ground was less than three feet. Three feet! Still, we couldn't do it.

The old Maytag was built the way they "used to make 'em" and was far too heavy for us kids just to lift it the three or so feet to the safety of the porch.

By now we were too panicked to place two planks from the edge of the porch to the ground and simply roll the machine up. We probably would have figured this out eventually; unfortunately for us, our parents came home before that brain storm hit.

Using planks was precisely what my father did when he got home. To their credit, our folks were not too angry about the machine. I believe it was because we told them some falsehood about how the washer came to be on the ground. "Aliens from outer space had dropped by to do their laundry and accidentally knocked the machine off the porch," we said.

CHAPTER 25: ADULT BASIC EDUCATION

In the late '60s, our great government took it upon themselves to undertake the education of the masses. Even rural hamlets such as our very own were to be affected. The Education Co-op of Cherokee County hired a teacher in the form of Mrs. Dora Griffith. Mrs. Griffith was not exactly a stranger to us, but as the years wore on, she came to be like family. That kind of thing happens when you are involved with a community for twelve long years.

The Education Co-op was to oversee the project for our area. The project? Adult Basic Education. Yep! The members of our community were about to be "edumacated." It was determined that the most suitable place to conduct classes would be the church.

Every Monday and Wednesday evening at 6:00 PM the group gathered to be "learnt." The students included uncles N. E., Claude and Hadie; aunts Jeffie, Louisiana and Odessa; cousins Arthur Lee, Lula Bee, and a few other occasionals. This latter group was a most truant bunch. They hardly ever showed up.

The core group consisted of Hadie, Claude, N. E., Monel, Odie, Jeffie, and Odessa. We youngsters had to attend, too, since our parents dared not leave us young teenagers home alone. So, on class nights there we sat: Jefffie Mae, Chee-Chee, Sister Girl, Big Sister and I, right there with the "old heads," as we fondly labeled the adults.

We didn't really mind since it gave us an opportunity to socialize with each other and do homework. Besides, on Wednesday evenings everyone participated in the little party held during break time; we got to do the food preparation and service. In the winter we made hot chocolate on the old gas heater at the back of the church. This heater was huge, about four feet long by three feet wide, and stood about four feet off the floor. The heater could get very hot, the vents on the top providing an excellent surface for heating food and beverages.

The menu generally consisted of hot chocolate or Kool-Aid and cream-filled sandwich cookies. You remember the kind—you could buy about 200 of them for around a dollar. They were nothing but fat, sugar and flour, in that order. I wouldn't be caught eating one now, but back then they were manna to us. In the warmer months we made buckets of Kool-Aid, which the old heads still called by its older trade name of "poly-pop." We'd eat and drink for about thirty minutes, then resume class. We teenagers often participated in the lessons, but most often we were content to do our own thing.

A-B-E continued for twelve years, long enough for everyone in the group to graduate; you'd have thought they would have finished sooner, but I don't believe any of them did. They weren't dumb or even senile (yet) by any means. In fact, both Jeffie and Hadie laid claim to having been educators themselves, way back in their younger years. The two taught school back in the early to mid-1900s.

The certification for teachers is vastly different now from then. Back then you could go to school for a year or so and hang out your shingle. I imagine it was sufficient just to know a bit more than the pupils. This is not to discount their attainments, though, since it is a fact that several of the clan did indeed receive at least some education from the nearest normal school.

The point is, they were more than adequately intelligent to have easily graduated in two or three years—max. I think they dragged it out so Miss Dora could keep coming to County Line. She liked us and we liked her. Furthermore, we always suspected that she and Uncle Claude had a bit of a thing going on. Nothing ever came of it, though. He was still married.

On the very first day of school, Miss Dora had gathered all the students in the grade level they felt they should start with. Most of the group started out in the second or third grade. The whole community was supportive of the A-B-E, even those who rarely attended. This was a federally-funded program, so there was the occasional administration "check-up." Uncle Sam's interest had to be protected, after all.

On these occasions the local co-op director would pay a visit, always providing plenty of warning. Miss Dora would ask all in the community to please attend and be counted. Without fail, everyone who could did come out. The Fearsome Five were counted in the number of A-B-E attendees. It didn't seem to matter that our average age was thirteen or that we were all in regular school—we were counted anyway. It would be a shame to start a federal investigation at this late date, so I won't name names, but I am fairly sure that Mr. So & So knew better.

Every little bit helps, I guess, and it didn't hurt us to go to A-B-E. No knowledge is ever wasted, and we did learn a lot, sometimes more from the stories the old heads told as they recounted events from the distant past than from the actual lessons. The "real" students learned, too, in spite of their often wandering thoughts and habitual wool-gathering. Case in point: one evening Miss Dora was instructing the class in proper sentence structure. She wanted her students to be able to aptly identify noun, verb, adjective, and so forth. This lesson, well within the capabilities of these students, in fact, was rather easy for them.

Miss Dora had the class on a roll. She would read a sentence like, "The tree stood by the sea." The chosen student responded with what she had taught, "Subject-tree, verb-stood, noun-sea." "Right you are," Miss Dora sang out.

Next. "The small ball rolled down the hall." Another student gave the answer, "Subject-*ball*, verb-*rolled*, noun-*hall*." I guess the rhyming nature of the sentences made them more engaging; either that or she was making a plug for Dr. Seuss. That was basically all there was to it. Miss Dora wasn't asking them to determine objects, participles, adjectives, adverbs and the like, just your basic noun-verb-noun.

The recitation continued. Every time a randomly selected student answered correctly Miss Dora would say, "Right you are," as she always did.

Finally, everyone had been called on except for Uncle N. E. The selection ceased being random at this point; it was flat-out his turn. He didn't know it, though, because he was busy gathering wool. Uncle N. E. was somewhat hard of hearing, even way back then, so perhaps that is why he had an altered perception of what was going on in the class. I lean more toward the "wool gathering" theory myself.

Miss Dora read the sentence for him, diction, articulation, locution, pitch, etc. All perfect. She couldn't have delivered it any more clearly.

"The cat sat by the fat rat," she read, pausing to look at Uncle N. E. "Mr. N. E. What about that one?"

Uncle N. E. hastily put his wool aside, pondered a moment and replied without missing more than a few beats. Uncle N. E. cleared his throat.

"I wouldn't say, 'The cat sat by the fat rat.'" Everyone listened politely as Uncle N. E. continued. "I would say, 'The cat ate the fat rat.'"

The class, suddenly animated, began to laugh uproariously, Miss Dora included. She at least tried valiantly, though vainly, to suppress her giggles as she explained to N. E. that the task was not to make the sentence logical but to simply identify its parts.

Uncle N. E. looked around sheepishly (at least he got something for his wool-gathering) at his classmates laughing at him. He tried to redeem himself by claiming that he just hadn't heard the instructions correctly. This lie did not wash! Everyone knew better.

Finally, Uncle N. E. conceded defeat and joined in the laughter himself. This incident occurred some twenty-five years ago and remains one of our favorite stories.

CHAPTER 26: THE MORE THINGS CHANGE

The other day I was outside under the huge oak tree on the south side of my parents' house. Pete was doing his thing with the barbeque pit, with me assisting. Pete's boys, P. J. and Alfred, and my girls, Elia and Sherrell, were running around, being kids and all.

I wasn't terribly busy at the pit; Pete didn't need much help. I was free to watch the kids as they played, occasionally threatening them when they got out of hand. I'd been watching them for half an hour or so when it dawned on me what game they were trying to play.

I grinned to myself as I realized the kids were playing "hide-and-go-seek." Boy, did this bring back memories. The only thing was, they weren't playing it right. They seemed disorganized, following no rules whatsoever. Obviously, they had not learned this game from Pete and me. We would have taught them the correct way to execute the components of the game. I did notice, though, that they got the name right. We always called it "hide-and-go-seek;" other kids leave out the "go," simply calling the game "hide-and-seek." How unimaginative!

P. J. was "it." I watched closely as he covered his face with his hands and began the count. 1, 2, 3, 4 . . . on up to 10. Where in the world did he learn to do it this way? P.J.'s cadence was all wrong, monotonous and boorrrring! He was also using the wrong counting cues. Ugh. I had work to do.

The hiders were even worse. Alfred, Elia, and Sherrell apparently had little idea what the word "hide" means. Their interpretation meant hiding in plain sight. P. J. was peeking anyway, so even if they had found a good place to hide, he would have spotted them.

I got Pete's attention, pointing out our kids' game problems. He readily agreed that something must be done.

P. J. was "it" again. It hadn't taken two or three minutes for him to find the hiders, choose another "it," and promptly get caught again himself.

This game was going nowhere. Why, when we played "hide-and-go-seek" in our young years the game went on for an hour or more. We played at night, fearlessly employing all kinds of wonderful hiding places. We hid in the corn crib, behind the cherry tree, on top of the tractor shed. It didn't matter how high or how dangerous the place was, if we wanted a good hiding place, we sought one out. No matter what!

Here were these kids hiding in plain view, in full daylight no less, counting all wrong, and if that wasn't enough—they cheated.

I called out to P. J. It took a while to get his attention; he was busy counting again 1, 2, 3 . . . 10.

"P. J.," I called again.

"Ma'am?" At least he'd learned something.

"Come over here, all of you." The other kids watched with interest as P. J. ran my way, hesitating to join him as he trotted to me.

"Let me teach y'all how to play 'hide-and-go-seek.'"

P. J. quickly agreed to my tutelage. "First," I began slowly, not wanting to lose my students to confusion. "You count like this." The old cadence came back without a hitch. I hadn't sung out the count in years and years, yet here I was: "Five ten, fifteen twenty, twenty-five thirty, thirty-five forty." On I went, soon reaching one hundred, calling the count in the sing-song voice we'd used as kids. There was an unmistakable rhythm to the count when done this way. The numbers were sung out in groups of two with a slight pause following the second number.

I continued my lessons. "You don't peek while the other kids are hiding," I admonished, "and you have to call out a warning just before you set out to find the hiders." P. J. and the others listened raptly as I instructed them on the fine art of game playing. Finally, we were ready to try my way. I would be "it."

I went to the corner of the house and faced in so that I couldn't see anything without turning my head. I didn't have to cheat anyway, I could easily hear which way they were going as they loudly scrambled around the yard, frantically hunting for good hiding places.

Still got work to do, I thought to myself as I finished up my count.

"Ninety-fiiivvee, one huuunnndred!" After a brief pause I continued. "All not hid better call out." This gave the last of the hiders time to quickly position themselves in their places.

It took maybe twenty seconds for me to find my girls and the boys. I was going to have to teach them about hiding places.

After tagging Alfred "it," I took Elia by the hand, running with her as I dragged her to a wonderful hiding place. Elia was the youngest of the group, not quite five, and I didn't feel I was being biased by helping her. I installed my daughter under the cover of the riding lawn mower, told her not to move or say anything and moved away.

I watched the proceedings from my spot by the barbeque pit. P. J. was "it" again. This time, he used my counting technique, almost perfectly emulating the cadence. I was proud.

They still couldn't hide worth a flip, but I wasn't about to show these clumsy youngsters any of the spots we used to hide in. I was afraid they'd break a leg or something, so I left well enough alone.

EPILOGUE

When I wrote these stories, I realized even then how very fortunate I was to have lived this life. It was certainly not always easy. In fact, by today's standards, some would deem it quite difficult. By my standards, though—and with an even fuller appreciation for the eternal impact growing up in County Line has had on my life—it seems quite the blessing. I wouldn't be the woman I am without these experiences. To those who may argue that better circumstances might have created a better woman, I say, "Probably so. But, she wouldn't be me, and how could I be anyone but who I am?" The me who is, will simply have to do.

Many of the "Biscuit" stories still bring smiles and laughter as I recall them. Some do not. When I wrote this book, our family circle was intact and even then, I knew it would not always be so. The young are capable of very strong delusions, however, and so I kept right on insisting to myself that we would always be just as we were then. The passage of time does one thing for certain—it clarifies reality and rips away even the most tightly woven curtains of fanciful delusions. Things change, lives change, people change . . . and now, here we are in the grips of COVID-19. All our lives are changing. Even the way we die is, by necessity, changing.

Change presents interesting dilemmas. When changes press upon us, we have to ask ourselves, "Do we move with the flow of inevitable events, or do we hang onto the solid, anchoring boulders of the past? Boulders of good character and values that are rooted in Biblical principles are present all around us. Sometimes we choose to move swiftly past them, even as the ebbs and eddies remind us that there is something solid nearby, something that we cannot and should not ignore. We follow the convenient and neglect the necessary. For those who feel as I do about our community, it is vitally important to embrace the necessary. And, it is necessary to embrace the future even as we cling to the very best of the past—our experiences, our memories, our learning, and our lives. Yes! We hang onto those, too. At any cost, we hold tight to the heritage we are fortunate to have.

We are blessed to still live in, near, or have access to our ancestral community. Even so, many of us have already learned that it is more about the people than it is about the place. From past to present, I am grateful for both the people and the place!

APPENDIX

Dictionary for Black Folks from the South

A'ion—na'ion: This means it is better to have "any one" than to have "nary a one." So a'ion beats na'ion.

Bits: Something to put in a horse's mouth to make him behave. Or currency. 2 bits = one quarter, 4 bits = fifty cents and so on. I surmise from that information that a "bit" is 12.5 cents.

Broughans: Refers to the company which manufactured the heavy, usually black, lace-up work boots men and sometimes women all over the South wore years ago. These days it is considered a friendly insult to have one's footwear referred to as "broughans."

Can't start it nowhere: Translation: the object cannot be found. Example: "I wonder what went with my red hat, I can't start it nowhere?" Now, do you get it?

Cheerrin: Refers to one's offspring, otherwise known as children.

Fell off: Lost weight. "So and so sure did fall off, didn't she?"

Fixin' to: About to do something. As in, "I'm fixin' to go to town."

Haints: Ghosts. Plain and simple. A mispronunciation of the word "haunts" used as a noun.

High sheriff: Refers to the local sheriff as opposed to his underlings (deputies). The "high" sheriff was the big man around the county. For years the "high" sheriff of Nacogdoches County was John Lightfoot. Today Sheriff Jason Bridges wears that title, although I have never heard him referred to as "high."

Hope: Past tense of help as in help, hope, have hope.

I swanee: Indicates amazement. "I declare" is similar, but "I swanee" could mean anything from "I don't believe this happened" to "I believe, but I don't understand how it happened" to "I see that it happened, and I see how it happened, I just don't give a damn."

In soak: Means having an item in hock (pawned). If someone's land was soaking, it rarely related to how much rain had fallen on it. Rather, it related to hard times that may have fallen on its owner.

Jick: Someone who loves to drink. Not necessarily an alcoholic, though a jick could very well be an alcoholic. If not now, then later. I surmise that this is a gross mispronunciation and adulteration of the bartending term "jigger." I believe that the word jigger was misunderstood and thus later mispronounced or perhaps shortened by folks too lazy to enunciate. In other words, people said "jig" for "jigger." No doubt the term was further adulterated from jig to jick. Therefore, a person who was out drinking was said to be out "jicking," jick being the noun and jicking the verb. There is occasional use of the term "jickish," I guess that being an adjective explaining someone's tendency to jick. The tenses for this word are as follows: jick, jick, jicked. As in, I jick occasionally. I will jick in the future and almost everyone I know has jicked from time to time. For some it is in fact a semi-permanent state of consciousness. (Or unconsciousness, depending upon the extent of the "jickship.")

Jury: Gross mispronunciation of the word "jewelry."

Lab: A private place in which to undertake certain subjects of research. In other words, an "outhouse."

Make out like: To pretend or indicate something that may or may not be true. Example: "He made out like he was coming home this week."

Nappy: This really needs no explanation. If you're of African-American descent (even a little bit), you already know perfectly well what nappy means. If you aren't and you don't, I advise that you find someone with curly locks and ask them.

On my hands: If someone said they didn't want so and so or such and such "on their hands," it meant they were attempting to absolve themselves of any guilt by association. That is to say that he or she was making an effort to make sure they were not guilty of any wrongdoing toward the person (usually people or perhaps events) whom they were trying to keep "off their hands." For example: if someone were close to dying and a relative came to visit, it could be said that the relative showed up at that particular time because they did not want to suffer any recriminations from God or other family members for neglecting the dying party. They wished to assure themselves and others that they had "done all they could" and therefore had no guilt or "blood" on their hands. Thus, they kept the unfortunate soul "off their hands."

Put something on him/her or **got something on him/her**: This most assuredly refers to voodoo-ism. To have something "put on you" means that you have come under the influence of a spell of some kind. These were usually bad spells, and this phrase is often used to explain the otherwise unexplainable, such as why a previously faithful spouse suddenly "takes up with" wild women/men.

Rat: Bear with me on this one. Rat is a varmint for sure; it is also a mistake on the word "right." Let me illustrate: my four-year-old daughter Elia was waking from her nap one day. Elia and my mother get along famously, but Elia sometimes feels it is her duty to correct my mother's grammar. (A lot of information for this glossary came from my mother, so I needn't justify why my child felt compelled to do this.)

Anyway, my mother was teasing Elia when she said, "I put the 'rat' over there." She deliberately said "rat" to see if Elia would wake on up and respond. Elia just lay there. My mother repeated her statement. Elia remained silent.

My mother again attempted to elicit a response. "Is that correct, Elia? Am I supposed to say 'rat' there?" Elia opened one sleepy eye and whispered, "No."

"What am I supposed to say?" mom foolishly asked.

"You're supposed to say mouse."

Seed: Past tense of see. "I seed him on the way to work." As in see, seed, seed.

Set 'em up to you: Paying back a favor. My theory as to the origin of this saying is this: In the olden days people went to saloons to quench their thirst. (Now they go to bars.) Anyway, the bartender "set up the drinks." So, it is reasonable to assume that to "set 'em up to you" actually refers to buying someone a drink.

Sho: Mispronunciation of the word "sure," as in "I sho is glad to see you." Or, "Sho 'nuff, you don't mean." In this case the use of those phrases expresses mild disbelief.

Smut: Not necessarily the stuff that the truly dirty-minded ole men read. The smut of this reference is the black matter found in the stove pipe or up the chimney flue, otherwise known as soot. Graying men and women in the South (and elsewhere no doubt) mixed this "smut" with Vaseline or some other grease and smeared it in their hair. This was the first "Miss Clairol." It worked pretty well, but pillowcases caught the blues or, more aptly, the blacks.

Sunt: Past tense of send (way past; as in send, sunt, have sunt).

Toe sack: Potato sack, used interchangeably with croaker sack. These are the heavy burlap bags potatoes and other vegetables used to come in.

Uhh dee! Uh oh, you done did it now: "Uhh dee" means you've been caught doing something you should not have been caught doing. This expression was most often uttered by siblings of the offender, though anyone who caught the miscreant could exclaim "uhh dee." It's just that one's brothers and sisters were always around and therefore more likely to catch you doing something.

What went with . . . ?: Translation: whatever happened to the person or object? Such as, "I wonder whatever went with old John boy?" This phrase goes well with the next one, especially when referring to objects.

Why: Not "why" like you might think. This usage is pronounced "wie" or "Yy." It is a mild exclamation. Example: "Why, I never did know the truth of the matter."

Grammatical Missteps

The following may be examples of speech impediments rather than true "grammatical" errors. But we will make no distinction here.

Ast: Again, let's keep it simple. "I ast you to get me some water." Translation: "I asked you to get me some water."

Go: Of course, this is an action verb meaning to get from one place or activity to another; it is also a verb meaning to tell lies— not just any ole kind of lie, but big hulking lies. Example: "So and so sure can *go* can't he?" (Be sure to emphasize the word go.)

Han'cha'cuff: A square of material, usually of cotton or cotton blend, used to deposit one's tears or other secretions.

Hoopie: A vehicle in less than perfect running condition, usually old and perhaps dented and rusty, maybe with missing parts such as fenders, bumpers, etc.

Kang: Jack, Queen, Kang. Princess Di will never be queen but Prince Charles will most probably one day be the "kang" of England.

Ne'mind: Never mind, plain and simple. (I don't mean to tell you "never mind;" rather, that is what "ne'mind" means.)

Scrent, scrait, screet: "I don't have the scrent to walk scrait down the screet." Translation: "I don't have the strength to walk straight down the street."

Screw: Some folks with more serious speech impediments pronounce "stew" as "screw." This reminds me of the cook who remarked that he had to hurry home because he had to "screw" a chicken. I hope he meant stew.

Stand up in the road: This is actually used as an adjective (I guess). It is a term used to denote a rather sorry individual as such. Generally, this phrase is used teasingly, and it may also mean that someone is simply too old or too big to be exhibiting the particular behavior which caused them to be called a "big stand up in the road." Example: "That gal ain't nothin' but a big ole stand up in the road. She's too sorry to pour piss out of a boot." If you recall the story of Maye and Byrd operating on the frog you will remember that when I asked Byrd how old they were when they performed this surgery her reply was, "I was just a kid, but Maye was a 'big ole stand up in the road.'" I suppose this phrase was first used when speaking about cows and other such creatures. Anyone who has ever lived in or visited or even "heard tell of" the goings on of the country will realize that cattle are the ultimate example of "big stand up in the roads." A cow will let you run your car right up next to her and never move. Then when you decide it is safe to speed up and drive around her (because it is plain to see this animal is not about to move), she decides to up and run right in front of you. So, cows are "stand up in the roads," or is it "stands up in the roads"? In any case, cows are those, and so are some people.

Swange: A mispronunciation (gross) of the word "singe." To singe something means to use a flame (fire) to burn off the remaining down, feathers, hair, fur, or fluff from an animal after it has been plucked. It is part of the "dressing" process. "Dressing," then, is the term used to describe what happens to chickens, turkeys, and other edibles before they arrive at the table. If the cook mentioned above lived in the country and raised his own chickens he would have "swanged" his chicken before he "screwed" it.

Ethnic Phraseology

Colored: What we were before we became "Negroes," just after emancipation. (Before that, we were—and sometimes still are—called something else entirely.)

Negroes: What we became after we stopped being colored.

Black: After being colored-Negroes we became black and proud. Actually, we were always proud, it just needed saying. James Brown said it loud!

African-American: What we always were.

ACKNOWLEDGMENTS

Kenneth L. Untiedt acknowledges the work of Emily Townsend, graduate assistant finishing her master's degree in English and Creative Writing at SFA who assisted him in editing; Ron Chrisman, Director of UNT Press and the rest of the staff at UNT Press, especially Karen DeVinney; the folks at the Consortium who distribute the books; Brian Murphy, the Dean of the College of Liberal and Applied Arts, and Steve Bullard, the Provost and Vice-President of Academic Affairs at SFA; Charlotte Blacksher, the TFS Office Secretary and Treasurer. I have enjoyed my time as Secretary-Editor of the TFS, and I consider it a privilege to have served this organization for the last sixteen years. Best wishes to all in the future.

The Texas Folklore Society acknowledges and appreciates the years at Stephen F. Austin State University, brought there by F. E. (Ab) Abernethy, dedicated folklorist and English professor, who wrote the history of the Society in three volumes—in addition to editing the folklore volumes published from 1971 to 2004; Kenneth L. Untiedt, who followed; Dean Brian Murphy of Liberal and Applied Arts; Provost and Vice President of Academic Affairs Steve Bullard, for the support given us over the years. We look forward to continuing to work with the University of North Texas Press as our publisher and the Texas A&M University Press Consortium as our distributor from our new home at Tarleton State University.

INDEX

M
Mama fixing hair, 190–192
Mama's green thumb, 137–142
Maytag washer, 221–223
McCray, Fred, 9–11
Mister-Brother Ed, 87
Morrisette, Jessie, 50–51, 162–163, 175
Murphy (family dog), 151–153

N
Nacogdoches, Texas, 2, 91

R
Rabid dog, 151–153

S
Sand rollers, 195–196
Sassafras tea expedition, 129–134
Snake and Sister Girl, 150

T
Tenchie's 1972 Dodge, 28–32
Tires (automobiles), 197–198

U
Uncle Hadie, 160, 162–163, 165–170
Upshaw, Alvin (Pete), 80–85, 111–118, 144–145, 215–217, 222–223
Upshaw, Beatrice, 3, 5, 11–14
Upshaw, Claude, 86–103, 161–162
Upshaw, Faye Eddie, 181–183
Upshaw, Gus, 20–21, 109–111, 118–121, 124, 204–205
Upshaw, Guss, 6–8, 13
Upshaw, Leota, 137–142
Upshaw, Marceline (Byrd), 52–55, 123, 134, 149–150, 178–183, 207–209, 216
Upshaw, Marilyn (Sister Girl), 20–22, 80, 82, 103–104, 108–109, 112, 123,
    138–141, 144–147, 148–153
Upshaw, Marion, 2
Upshaw, Maye Florence, 207–212
Upshaw, Maye, 74–76, 123–124, 131–133, 159, 204–205, 207–212
Upshaw, Neal (N. E.), 162, 201–202, 225, 228–229
Upshaw, Odessa, 181–183, 185–189
Upshaw, Rev. John Gillis, 79–83

W
Wash day, 219–222